THE GLASS ROOF

THE
GLASS ROOF

Virginia Woolf as Novelist

By James Hafley

NEW YORK

RUSSELL & RUSSELL · INC

1963

FIRST PUBLISHED IN 1954
REISSUED, 1963, BY RUSSELL & RUSSELL, INC.
BY ARRANGEMENT WITH THE UNIVERSITY OF CALIFORNIA PRESS
L. C. CATALOG CARD NO: 64—10389

PRINTED IN THE UNITED STATES OF AMERICA

FOR MY MOTHER
MAE NEWBERRY HAFLEY

ACKNOWLEDGMENT

To each of the many persons who assisted me with this study, I am sincerely grateful. It is a special privilege for me to thank Myron F. Brightfield, Mark Schorer, and James R. Caldwell, of the University of California, whose help was particularly abundant and indispensable.

J. H.

CONTENTS

The huge uproar is in my ears. It sounds and re-
sounds under this glass roof like the surge of a
sea.

Neville

"And then——" she began again. But a great
lorry came crashing down the street. Something
rattled on the table. The walls and the floor
seemed to tremble. She parted two glasses that
were jingling together. The lorry passed; they
heard it rumbling away in the distance.

"And the birds," she went on. "The nightin-
gales, singing in the moonlight?"

Sara Pargiter

CHAPTER I

INTRODUCTION

As THE NUMBER of books and essays concerning the novels of
Virginia Woolf increases, so also does the number of
conflicting opinions concerning those novels. But perhaps at the basis of—and more important than—the critics' other
disagreements is their lack of agreement simply as to what Virginia Woolf's novels are about. Thus, for example, Joan Bennett
finds no metaphysical system in the novels, but only Virginia
Woolf's own "sense of values";[1] Bernard Blackstone speaks of
Chinese quietism, mysticism, romanticism, and "an enquiry
which is strictly metaphysical";[2] David Daiches notices the influence of Bergson, Proust, Joyce, and Freud;[3] Floris Delattre too
sees the influence of Bergson and Proust, but no important influence of Joyce or Freud;[4] F. C. Frierson recognizes impressionism, but no real thought at all;[5] Winifred Holtby says that Virginia Woolf was not significantly influenced by Bergson, Joyce,
and Proust, but that she was "a good Platonist";[6] Maxime Chastaing discovers traditional British empiricism;[7] Deborah Newton
can find no consistently reasoned philosophy;[8] Joseph Warren
Beach and Rebecca West agree that "Virginia Woolf is a philosopher writing fiction. . . . In short, she is a poet";[9] J. Isaacs finds
"a very profound effect" of Pater, and William James' influence;[10] Ruth Gruber, a typical "melancholy English" philosophy.[11] These distinguished critics—and many others—have
written about Virginia Woolf with real insight and valuable dis-
cernment; yet it is only natural that their divergent findings
should result in equally divergent interpretations and assess-
ments of her novels.

This study, then, is an attempt to explicate Virginia Woolf's
novels, through a general, factual examination of the development of her ideas as they are given definition by her technique.

The pattern of this development will be set forth in the light of Virginia Woolf's intellectual surroundings and influences, in order that her work may be placed in the historical frame to which it belongs. It is my contention that the novels, taken in their chronological order, reveal a constant and organic development of thought, and consequently of form; that the technical development from the second novel, *Night and Day,* to the third, *Jacob's Room,* though more immediately obvious, is actually far less important and marked than later developments, despite the fact that most previous critics tend to regard it as the main artistic crisis in the novels. Therefore the nine novels will be examined in the order of their composition. Finally there will be a summary of the configuration of meaning traced in its development in the main body of this study. The result will be a detailed analysis of just what the novels try to do and how they try to do it—in short, a description based upon an examination of meaning.

With D. H. Lawrence, James Joyce, and Aldous Huxley, Virginia Woolf repudiated the positivistic realism that she felt to have characterized certain members of the preceding generation of English novelists. Like her contemporaries, she sought and found a new way of looking at life—an original perspective, a vision of experience. Expression of this philosophical perspective in art required a new formal perspective as well, but it was at first the thought that necessitated the form, and not so much the form that determined the thought. Although much attention has been given to the thought of Lawrence, of Joyce, of Huxley, Virginia Woolf has been noticed and valued mainly as a superb stylist and writer of English prose. Yet she, profoundly as any of her contemporaries, was concerned with the philosophical as well as the purely formal problems of her art. That art—although this is arguable—may be not so great as Lawrence's or Joyce's or even Huxley's: it may be that Virginia Woolf succeeded so well because the goal she set herself was easier to reach.

What is important is that she was not simply an impressionist, a person with nothing to say who said it beautifully, but a serious artist whose main purpose in her novels was to convey a unified vision of life and experience. It seems to have been her misfortune, however, as perhaps it was Sterne's, to express herself so well—to convey this vision in so interesting a way—that many of her readers have often paid too much attention to how she writes, and too little to what she means. Again like Sterne, it was her misfortune to command a philosophical perspective that the novel proper is perhaps not suited to formalize; therefore, rather than sacrifice vision to alien form, she managed to achieve a formal perspective that could, and in her best work did, express that vision perfectly. The content—and that alone—can be used to justify its form; but the content must first be understood through an examination of its form.

To such an understanding of her thought and art, the external facts of Virginia Woolf's life—and they alone, unfortunately, are available at the present time—are not particularly important. If and when her diaries are published in their entirety and her definitive biography is written, the student of her novels will have a great deal more with which to work; at present he can only gather together some of the relatively few known facts and speculate about their relationship to her work.

Virginia Woolf was born Adeline Virginia Stephen on January 25, 1882, the third child of Leslie Stephen and his second wife Julia Prinsep Jackson Duckworth.[12] She was educated at home: choosing as she pleased from among the books in her father's large library; meeting such famous friends of his as George Meredith, Thomas Hardy, Henry James; learning the Greek alphabet from Walter Pater's sister. Her mother died in 1895, her father in 1904; both of them, but especially her father, influenced her work as well as her character in no small degree.[13]

After Leslie Stephen's death Virginia moved with her sister Vanessa (a painter and, in her drawings for Virginia Woolf's

books, her sister's best commentator) from Hyde Park Gate to
Bloomsbury. In 1912 she married the journalist and political
figure Leonard Woolf; they lived in Richmond until shortly after
World War I, and then returned to Bloomsbury, having begun
the Hogarth Press in 1917 with Leonard Woolf's winnings in
the Calcutta Sweepstakes. (This press rose from an amateurish
hobbyhorse for the young couple to become one of the significant
English publishing houses.)

Although she had lived elsewhere, and had indeed traveled
throughout Europe, Bloomsbury became Virginia Woolf's real
home. She herself became, most strangely, the center of the famous, perhaps the notorious, "Bloomsbury Group." Strangely,
because—although this has not been realized—she had intellectually very little of real importance in common with most of the
other "members," who included Roger Fry, Lytton Strachey,
Clive and Vanessa Bell, Raymond Mortimer, and possibly David
Garnett. Stephen Spender, having named these persons as the
core of the group, calls it "the most constructive and creative influence on English taste between the two wars."[14] Virginia Woolf
was, it would seem, simply a gracious hostess to this interesting
and variegated group of persons. In 1907, as a matter of fact, she
was not even that: the group met on Thursday evenings in her
large workroom, but she herself was usually very silent, torn between extreme shyness and silence and "sudden outbursts of
scathing criticism."[15] This, then, is one version of the "Bloomsbury
Group."

On the other hand, the Lord Keynes "Bloomsbury Group," as
it is revealed in his *Two Memoirs*,[16] was a Cantabrigian circle
passionately interested in metaphysical speculation and with
Moore's *Principia Ethica* as its bible; the conversations seem to
have been much like the one that opens Forster's *The Longest
Journey*. Although a superficial consideration of Moore's doctrine—emphasizing what Lord Keynes refers to as "timeless,
passionate states of contemplation and communion, largely un-

attached to 'before' and 'after' "—does suggest Virginia Woolf's "moments of being," the smallest amount of reflection makes evident a complete lack of correspondence between the two. In this group Virginia Woolf was a "silent partner" and, again, a hostess.

It will become more evident in the course of this study that Virginia Woolf was not intellectually in accord with "Bloomsbury"; it will also become apparent that her own dealings with and solutions to the problems discussed there were precisely her own, and not dependent upon this group of which she was socially at the center.

The Keynes "Bloomsbury Group" is the one that so provoked F. R. Leavis, who deplored its treatment of D. H. Lawrence, referred to it as "inimical to the development of any real seriousness," and asked, "Can one imagine . . . Leslie Stephen . . . being influenced by, or interested in, the equivalent of Lytton Strachey?"[17] And Leavis is not alone in his antipathy. What must be explained, however, is that Virginia Woolf's work is not "Bloomsbury" in any distasteful connotation of the word; that although she called herself a "highbrow" and a "snob," it was in her own sense of these terms and not in the sense in which they are applied to Bloomsbury by its detractors; that, above all, her thought—her philosophical perspective—can be neither defined nor detected as "Bloomsbury." T. S. Eliot has said that "Virginia Woolf was the centre, not merely of an esoteric group, but of the literary life of London. . . . With the death of Virginia Woolf, a whole pattern of culture is broken: she may be, from one point of view, only the symbol of it; but she would not be the symbol if she had not been, more than anyone in her time, the maintainer of it." Although Eliot does not deign to use the word "Bloomsbury," he mentions that the sufficient answer to that society's detractors "would probably be that it was the only one there was. . . . Any group will appear more uniform, and probably more intolerant and exclusive from the outside than it really is; and here, certainly, no subscription of orthodoxy was imposed. Had it, indeed, been a matter of limited membership and exclusive doctrine, it would not have attracted the exasperated attention of those who objected to it on these supposed grounds."[18]

In 1904, the same year in which she moved to Bloomsbury, Virginia Woolf began contributing critical reviews to the *Times Literary Supplement;* and about 1906 she wrote her first novel, *The Voyage Out,*[19] although it was not published until 1915. Besides nine novels, she wrote short stories, sketches, essays, lectures, biographies, feminist literature (of a special kind), and, with S. S. Koteliansky, translations from the Russian.

On March 28, 1941, Virginia Woolf drowned herself in the River Ouse on Sussex Downs, near which she had lived during the early part of World War II. She committed suicide neither because of depression over her last novel nor because she could not stand the thought of going on through another war, although both of these have been given as reasons for her death.[20] In fact, it is said that during the German blitz she helped give first aid, and that she continued (like Drake as the Armada approached) "to play bowls at Rodmell during the Battle of Britain, with Spitfires and Messerschmitts fighting, swooping and crashing round her."[21] Again, not only her last novel, but several of her novels, caused her nervous collapses because of her extremely self-critical nature. She did, indeed, dislike the ending of *Between the Acts,* her last novel, and she felt that the novel as a whole was below her standard; she also profoundly regretted that there should be another war, murmuring after a bomb had seriously damaged her London house that "every beautiful thing will soon be destroyed." But the reason for her suicide was the return of a mental condition from which she had suffered during part of the period at Richmond and from which she feared that she would not again recover. To Leonard Woolf she wrote: "I feel certain that I am going mad again. I feel we can't go through another of those horrible times. And I shan't recover this time. I hear voices and cannot concentrate on my work. I have fought against it, but cannot fight any longer. I owe all my happiness in life to you. You have been perfectly good. I cannot go on and spoil your life."[22] A coroner's inquest pronounced her death suicide "while the balance of her mind was disturbed." Since her death her husband has published *Between the Acts,* several volumes of her essays and sketches, one slim volume of her short stories, and a book of extracts from her diaries; there remain unpublished by far the greater part of the diaries and whatever letters and rejected fragments may exist.

The year 1915, in which Virginia Woolf's first novel, *The Voyage Out,* was published, is not a particularly useful date for the critic of her work, since this novel was evidently first written when she was twenty-four years old, some nine years before the time of its publication. It will perhaps be profitable, however, to begin by examining very briefly the state of the English novel from about 1905 to 1915, while keeping in mind Virginia Woolf's famous and remarkable assertion, which she admitted to be possibly "disputable," that "in or about December, 1910, human character changed."[23]

CHAPTER II

THE EARLY NOVELS

IF HUMAN CHARACTER changed in 1910, the English novel did not. Because King George V succeeded King Edward VII on the throne in that year, it soon became convenient to distinguish the "Georgian" from the "Edwardian" novel; but it is unlikely that by 1924, when Virginia Woolf made her statement about human character, she would have forgot that George became king in May, 1910, and not in December. The significance of December, 1910, has nothing to do with the novels then being published; nevertheless there are important differences between the Edwardian and the Georgian novel.

By 1905 all but two of the major Victorian novelists were dead, and those two—George Meredith and Thomas Hardy—were writing not novels but poetry. Mrs. Humphry Ward was writing mostly feministic novels between 1905 and 1915; and a more important novelist, George Moore, published *The Lake* in 1905 and only two novels—*The Brook Kerith* and *Héloïse and Abélard*—after that. Moore's main contribution during this period, and perhaps the most important of his works, was *Hail and Farewell*.

The novelists in full swing during the Edwardian period, and those who had a good start at that time, included Conrad, Wells, Bennett, Galsworthy, Forster, May Sinclair, Sheila Kaye-Smith, Maurice Hewlett, William Wymark Jacobs, Arthur Machen, Eden Phillpotts, Henry Handel Richardson, Algernon Blackwood, Sir Philip Gibbs, Hugh Walpole, Hilaire Belloc, G. K. Chesterton, William De Morgan, Robert Hichens, Leonard Merrick, J. D. Beresford, W. B. Maxwell, W. J. Locke, Somerset Maugham, and Ford Madox Ford.

Obviously, "Edwardian" loses even its chronological meaning if it is applied to all these writers; Ford Madox Ford, for example, did his best work well after 1910, and has nothing in common with, say, Wells. When Virginia Woolf spoke of the Edwardian novelists as "materialists" in "Mr. Bennett and Mrs. Brown," she had in mind the very popular but lesser novelists Wells, Galsworthy, and Bennett, and not at all Conrad and Forster.

"Georgian" is equally valueless as a descriptive term for the novelists of 1910–1936. The first of these decades saw the early work of such novelists as Lawrence, Joyce, Dorothy M. Richardson, Frank Swinnerton, Stella Benson, Rebecca West, Victoria Sackville-West, C. E. Montague, Norman Douglas, E. M. Tomlinson, Compton Mackenzie, Wyndham Lewis, Ronald Firbank, E. M. Delafield, St. John G. Ervine, Gilbert Cannan, W. L. George, James Stephens, and Henry Green, many of whom are, of course, still writing. In the 1920's some of the more important beginning novelists were Aldous Huxley, Elizabeth Bowen, Rose Macaulay, Maurice Baring, T. F. Powys, Sarah Millin, Gladys Stern, Margaret Kennedy, Louis Golding, Liam O'Flaherty, and David Garnett; in the 1930's, Evelyn Waugh, Graham Greene, Christopher Isherwood, Sylvia Townsend Warner, J. B. Priestley, and—of some historical importance— A. J. Cronin, whose *Hatter's Castle* in 1931 is said by devotees of naturalism to have helped "restore the English novel to sanity"[1]—the sanity, that is to say, of the Edwardians.

And whatever else Wells, Galsworthy, and Bennett may have been, they were most certainly sane.

Most people in this world seem to live "in character"; they have a beginning, a middle, and an end, and the three are congruous one with another and true to the rules of their type. You can speak of them as being this sort of people or that. They are, as theatrical people say, no more (and no less) than "character actors."[2]

That is an Edwardian sentiment, and this is the corresponding Georgian sentiment:

Who in the world can give anyone a character? Who in this world knows anything of any other heart—or of his own? I don't mean to say that one cannot form an average estimate of the way a person will behave. But one cannot be certain of the way any man will behave in every case—and until one can do that a "character" is of no use to anyone.[3]

These passages, especially the second, are distorted by having been removed from their contexts; nevertheless they serve to exemplify Edwardian and Georgian points of view, and to justify, with countless other examples, Virginia Woolf's assertion that human character changed in 1910. Irene, in Galsworthy's *Forsyte Saga,* is a mystery to many of the other people in that book, but never to the author or the reader; Jacob, in Virginia Woolf's *Jacob's Room,* is a mystery to his friends, the author, the reader, and himself.

The Edwardians saw people as simple, whole, definable; the Georgians saw them as complex, diverse, ineffable. But not until about 1915 did Georgian novels—in this sense—begin to appear; and even after 1925 Galsworthy, Bennett, and Wells continued to write Edwardian novels, although Galsworthy began to reflect certain Georgian tendencies.

Several different nonliterary events were responsible for this change in perspective. Since human character had changed, the Edwardian novels were no longer satisfactory to young writers. The novels of Henry James began to be appreciated; Freud's writings began to appear in English translation very shortly after 1910; in December, 1910, the Post-Impressionist Exhibition had opened at the Grafton Galleries and had shown, in another art, a whole new way of looking at people and life; the ideas of Henri Bergson and of William James started to gain attention in England shortly after 1907[5]—for all these reasons some people began to question the validity and the reality of life as the Edwardians depicted it and Herbert Spencer glossed it.

Added to these influences was a literary event of which the importance cannot be exaggerated—the impact of Dostoevski.

It is not quite correct to speak of the Russian novel as having influenced the Georgians, because the Russian novel influenced the Edwardians as well. Galsworthy, in a letter written to Edward Garnett in 1914,[6] for example, refers to Tolstoi, Turgenev, Chekhov, and others as "the men we swear by," but he deplores Dostoevski and blames him for Lawrence's "faults." Certainly the Georgians' Tolstoi—and Tolstoi was one influence upon Virginia Woolf—was somewhat different from the Edwardians' Tolstoi; nevertheless they shared their admiration for him. Dostoevski belonged, for the most part, to the Georgians alone.

Turgenev, Dostoevski, and Tolstoi had been translated into English druing the 1880's, but not until after 1910 were the Russians admired and detested with the violence that runs through the years of World War I. Specifically, it was in 1912, when Constance Garnett began her excellent translation of Dostoevski,[7] that his and the other Russian novels really took hold of English readers. What the Georgians liked espceially about Dostoevski was not, as Galsworthy implied, a preoccupation with the physical, but his preoccupation with inner states— with the closely observed workings of people's minds—rather than with external facts, and, above all, his ability to convey what people feel as well as what they think and do. More than any other Russian, Dostoevski concerned himself with what Virginia Woolf called "soul":[8] with the feelings that can unite persons who think and act very differently from each other.

But this new perspective, if it was to be satisfactorily communicated, required a new technique. The Edwardian formulas rang false for the Georgians: they were too matter-of-fact, too pat; the innovations of Henry James and Conrad had made obvious the Edwardian limitations. James' insight and technical ability enabled him to produce novels that made all too evident Wells' and Galsworthy's slick emptiness; and these novels showed the Georgians that if they were to explore new territory they would have to forge new tools. The Russian novel, compared with that of the Edwardians and of James and Conrad,

seemed at first to lack significant form;" actually it showed that
form was a means of communication and that in successful art,
form was communication itself. Such an extraliterary event as
the Post-Impressionist Exhibition served to confirm this idea of
form as expression. By 1915 these intellectual and formal revalu-
ations were beginning to get themselves articulated in the English novel.

The Edwardians were represented in 1915 by such novels as
Wells' *The Research Magnificent,* Galsworthy's *The Freelands,*
and to a large extent by Somerset Maugham's impressive natu-
ralistic novel *Of Human Bondage.* Conrad's *Victory* also appeared. But one of the best novels of the year was Ford Madox
Ford's *The Good Soldier,* and it must—if it is to be assigned—be
labeled Georgian. Georgian also were Lawrence's *The Rainbow*—promptly banned, of course; Firbank's slight *Vainglory;*
and *Pointed Roofs,* the first volume of Dorothy M. Richardson's
roman-fleuve Pilgrimage, in which stream-of-consciousness technique made a conspicuous appearance. Joyce's *Portrait of the
Artist as a Young Man* was being published serially in the
Egoist.

The Edwardians continued to concern themselves with facts,
with improvement of social conditions, with clear-cut people in
a clear-cut world; the Georgians, asking question after question,
tried to probe beneath the surface of society and of human
character, down to where they felt that the real truth lay hidden.

They agreed to go right away. It would not matter if they did not
come back. They were indifferent to the actual facts.

"I suppose we ought to get married," he said, rather wistfully. It
was so magnificently free and in a deeper world, as it was. To make
public their connection would be to put it in range with all the things
which nullified him, and from which he was for the moment entirely
dissociated. If he married he would have to assume his social self.
And the thought of assuming his social self made him at once diffi-
dent and abstract. If she were his social wife, if she were part of that
complication of dead reality, then what had his under-life to do with

her? One's social wife was almost a material symbol. Whereas now she was something more vivid to him than anything in conventional life could be. She gave the complete lie to all conventional life, he and she stood together, dark, fluid, infinitely potent, giving the living lie to the dead whole which contained them.[10]

On one side, the "actual facts ... public ... social self ... dead reality ... material ... conventional life ... the dead whole"; on the other, "a deeper world ... under-life." Throughout *The Rainbow*, and throughout these Georgian novels in general, there is expressed the wish to strip away a dead outer covering, to cast off what is mere appearance, to find underneath—inside—the reality that has been hidden by a superimposed husk. To each novelist the "reality" was something different; each had to find and express it, therefore, in a new and sometimes an oblique manner; but each agreed with the others that the "reality" was there, waiting and needing to be found and expressed. The function of the artist, then, was not to reproduce "actual facts" faithfully—indeed, he must give them the lie—but to assert the validity of the "deeper world" and "under-life" as the basis of a living reality. The entire movement can be summed up as a new search for the old absolute, despite the fact that the Georgians usually expressed the absolute in relativistic terms. Each Georgian novelist had to find reality, to communicate it artistically; but in order to communicate it artistically, he had at the same time to justify it by means of form: thought and technique were therefore essentially the same problem for him. At first the Georgian novelists might either use accepted techniques to help them define their thought or adapt the techniques somewhat to the thought; eventually each novelist had to create new form from the very stuff of his thought—think up to form—since that thought "gave the lie" to conventional form as well as to conventional life.

Dorothy M. Richardson seems to have solved her problem immediately; her first novel is a departure from tradition in both thought and technique, and her last novel is exactly the same as her first. Her protagonist, Miriam, develops, to be sure; but this very development is the frame of the entire *roman-fleuve,* and that frame, in terms of form, remains static. Joyce and Lawrence, on the other hand, began by writing conventionally, so that a continual development of thought and technique can be traced through their novels; and so it is with the novels of Virginia Woolf.

The Voyage Out was published in 1915 by Duckworth. The action begins in October, 1908, and concludes in the following May. Externally the structure of this novel is completely conventional; it is narrated from the omniscient point of view that all the novels have in common; it contains description, narration, conventional thought transcription, and—predominantly—conversation between two or more of the characters. Its central story is that of Rachel Vinrace, a young and inexperienced girl whose practical education is taken in hand by the most powerful character of the novel, Helen Ambrose, at Santa Marina, a small town in Brazil to which they have come aboard the cargo ship *Euphrosyne* from London. Rachel is brought into a variety of experiences with a variety of people, falls in love with Terence Hewet, and, when she has just begun to emerge from her chrysalis into the life of a normal young woman, becomes ill and dies of a tropical fever.

Of Virginia Woolf's nine novels, *The Voyage Out* has received least care from the critics, who usually dismiss it as a "first novel," and whose opinions as to its meaning and worth differ considerably. Thus E. B. Burgum calls it a failure, and states its theme as "the hesitation a girl of spirit and breeding felt at yielding in marriage to one of the traditionally dominant sex."[11] He adds that after this "failure" Virginia Woolf never wrote of love again but only of middle age! On the other hand, W. H.

Mellers, in a piece of adverse criticism, says that it is one of the four novels that "will suffice to preserve Mrs. Woolf's reputation."[12] Again, whereas Pelham Edgar finds *The Voyage Out* masterly and says that since convention seems not to have hampered Virginia Woolf she had no justification for her later experiments,[13] David Daiches believes that "there seems to be a struggle between the form of [*The Voyage Out*] and the content. Social events and situations that seem to come straight out of Jane Austen merge into moods and dimnesses that would have baffled Jane completely."[14]

Such phrases as Daiches' "moods and dimnesses" are typical of some Virginia Woolf criticism (though not of Daiches' own); to say that a novel has "moods and dimnesses," and then to decide that there is an incompatibility between its form and its content, is perhaps to do little. Of course a novel about which nothing more precise than this can be said deserves to be dismissed as a "first novel"; *The Voyage Out,* however, seems not to be such a book. At a first acquaintance with the novel, the reader is inclined to agree with Daiches' conclusions; careful rereadings—in which the "dimnesses" become more and more illumined and illuminating—dispel those conclusions almost entirely.

Nearly every action, nearly every event in *The Voyage Out* is made to be symbolical. Thus there are two voyages: the voyage *out* from London to South America, and the voyage *in* from Santa Marina to a native camp on the bank of the Amazon. The first of these voyages, occupying the first six chapters of the novel, serves at once to set the stage and to suggest Rachel's voyage to an understanding of life and experience; the second, occurring shortly after the climax of the novel—shortly after Rachel and Terence fall in love—coincides with Rachel's voyage to an understanding of herself. The tragedy here is at once Rachel's death and her inability to unite her own world with the world around her. When she has come to an understanding of the world around her, Rachel first becomes puzzled about herself as an individual in this world. It is this dispute between the individual and society with which the novel is primarily concerned. Thus the Villa San Gervasio, where Rachel lives with Helen and Ridley Ambrose, represents the individual's world, and the hotel below it represents the social world.

In chapter viii Helen and Rachel go for a walk from the villa down to the hotel, where they have not been before. Walking around the outside terrace, they look into one window after another: dining room, kitchen, drawing room, lounge. Inside the lounge, the hotel's largest room, are Terence Hewet and his brilliant friend St. John Hirst; Hirst catches sight of the two onlookers, and the women flee. The reader, however, remains. In chapter ix the tour of rooms is continued: each bedroom holds its individual, but this unity is part of the diversity of the whole. The diversity itself, however, resolves into the unity of the hotel—as a structural unit, the social world is very similar to the individual world of the villa. Later Rachel goes on a personal tour of individual bedrooms in the hotel: she has grasped the world around her as a unit with various facets but must now come to grips with its diversity. She has seen the inhabitants of the hotel in the lounge, at a dance during which she herself plays the music for the dancers; now she begins to answer invitations to "Come and see my room." She must recognize the unit of people in terms of each member's individuality. This problem of communication appears in various ways throughout the novel.

When Rachel leaves the hotel and goes out into the sunlight, she finds a group of people united around a tea table. One of this group, Mrs. Flushing, invites Rachel to come for a trip along the Amazon, and Rachel accepts—thus beginning the catastrophe of the novel.

This second voyage, then—the voyage *in*—symbolizes Rachel's discovery of herself and her retirement into herself. Just as the

first voyage is compared to the voyages of Spanish and Elizabethan English adventurers—and Rachel's discovery compared
to theirs—so this second voyage is compared to that of an ex-
plorer named Mackenzie, who "had died of fever some ten years
ago, almost within reach of civilization . . . the man who went
farther inland than anyone's been yet."[15] Again, "they seemed to
be driving into the heart of the night, for the trees closed in
front of them. . . . The great darkness had the usual effect of
taking away all desire for communication by making their
words sound thin and small." Each incident of this journey has
its symbolic value in terms of the theme. The journey reaches its
climax in a love scene between Rachel and Terence, after which
both are silent and blissfully content in a story-book peace and
unity. Rachel, indeed, does not even see Mackenzie's hut when
it is pointed out to them and his story told. She is completely
absorbed in herself and in Terence. Love, marriage—these are
the words she savors as the journey continues inland and the
heat becomes more and more oppressive. " 'This is happiness,' "
she says. Rachel's is the typical tragic situation: the very thing
that is to redeem her—her love for Terence—is also to cause her
death. Love has not only helped Rachel to discover herself, but
has also led her to reject all outside herself. To see oneself as
reality and the social world as illusion, then, is fatal.

Terence—who is able to adapt his own world to the world outside himself—returns from the journey; Rachel remains in the
jungle of her world and denies the world outside. Finally, however, Rachel must lose even Terence, for despite their love he
cannot enter into her individual world. In the delirium that
results from her sickness Rachel does not know Terence; just
before her death she smiles and speaks to him, but it is then too
late.

The rift between Terence and Rachel begins when they argue
about whether or not they are to go to the hotel. Terence, of
course, wishes to have tea with Mrs. Thornbury in return for

her kindnesses: he wishes to bring his relationship with Rachel
to the social world. "He wanted other people; he wanted Rachel
to see him with them." Finally Rachel yields, goes to the hotel,
endures the congratulations. In the afternoon she starts to have
a severe headache; her final illness has begun.

Rachel is the central character of *The Voyage Out,* but
Terence Hewet's behavior—not Rachel's—is in accord with the
perspective. This novel would be pathos rather than tragedy if
Rachel's death were offered as the normal solution to the problem it presents. The last chapter makes clear the fact that
Rachel's attitude is wrong and Terence's right. St. John Hirst,
who has been Rachel Vinrace's counterpart throughout the
novel, is the key figure in the last pages. He comes back from
the villa to the hotel, over which Rachel's death has cast an
unnatural sobriety of mood. It is night when he arrives at the
hotel, and a storm—which comes to symbolize the "life itself"
against which both individual and social life are placed—contrasts with the hotel's guests gathered together in the lounge.
Gradually, despite their sorrow for Rachel, these people have
resumed their normal occupations: they are knitting, reading,
talking, playing chess. Hirst, who has walked from the villa
through the storm, feels suddenly quite secure when he looks
at them in the warm, comfortable room. He is turning from
Rachel's position to Terence's. The lightning flashes, and spreads
"a broad illumination over the earth." Conversation goes on, the
chess game concludes. "All these voices sounded gratefully in St.
John's ears as he lay half-asleep, and yet vividly conscious of
everything around him. Across his eyes passed a procession of
objects, black and indistinct, the figures of people picking up
their books, their cards, thei⁻ balls of wool, their work-baskets,
and passing him one after another on their way to bed." Neither
the individual world nor the social world is complete within itself; the two must blend together. Both are finite, but "life itself"
is one and infinite. Of this last there is only a suggestion in

Virginia Woolf's first novel; the problem of "life itself" will be explored later.

Hirst's relationship to Rachel and Terence's own position are both made clear in an earlier passage in the novel:

> Hewet proceeded to think.
>
> "The truth of it is that one never is alone, and one never is in company," he concluded.
>
> "Meaning?" said Hirst.
>
> "Meaning? Oh, something about bubbles—auras—what d'you call 'em? You can't see my bubble; I can't see yours; all we see of each other is a speck, like the wick in the middle of that flame. The flame goes about with us everywhere; it's not ourselves exactly, but what we feel; the world in short, or people mainly; all kinds of people. . . .
>
> "And supposing my bubble could run into someone else's bubble——"
>
> "And they both burst?" put in Hirst.
>
> "Then—then—then—" pondered Hewet, as if to himself, "it would be an e—nor—mous world."

The flame, Virginia Woolf is to say later, more clearly than she says it at the conclusion of this novel, may be put out, but the wick—the carrier of the flame—is there to be lighted again.

A popular attitude toward Virginia Woolf's novels is that of G. U. Ellis: "In Virginia Woolf, the isolated individual is seen from within. . . . The individual . . . remains a largely isolated creature, and, as a result, we get not an interpretation of human relationship, but the 'observation' of individual behaviour."[16] Again, Philip Henderson takes offense at Virginia Woolf's ignoring "the external world" which she fears and detests.[17] N. Elizabeth Monroe argues that Virginia Woolf is a great and serious artist but not a novelist; that she has no plot or character description; that she is not a success, because she ignores action, the will, and the outer world; that she plays with many ideas and values but accepts none.[18]

The Voyage Out would seem to refute each of these charges, although some of them surely apply to certain of the later novels.

What is important is to realize that Virginia Woolf could write novels with plots; that she could create "characters" in the traditional sense of that term—Helen Ambrose, Terence Hewet, St. John Hirst, Mrs. Paley, Evelyn Murgatroyd, Miss Allan, and Mr. Pepper are a few of the examples from this novel; that she could write about classes other than her own, and write about them well; that she could write dialogue—think of Mrs. Flushing, for example—completely appropriate to the persons who spoke it; that she could write about the individual in society; that, in short, if later on she chose not to do some of these things, it was evidently for a definite purpose, and not simply because she was unable to do them. Virginia Woolf did not write "that way" because she could not write "the right way" any more than Matisse paints "that way" because he cannot paint "the right way."

The Voyage Out is more important as a sign of what is to come than as a refutation of questionable statements about its successors. This novel contains the germs of many concepts later to be given full expression by Virginia Woolf, and it will be valuable next to consider some of these.

Terence Hewet is a novelist, and one of his speeches has been often quoted as pertinent to Virginia Woolf's later novels: " 'I want to write a novel about Silence . . . the things people don't say. But the difficulty is immense. . . . However, you don't care. . . . Nobody cares. Never mind. It's the only thing worth doing.' " But what no one seems to have noticed is the partial resemblance of this passage to one in Proust's *Le Temps retrouvé:* "Les vrais livres doivent être les enfants non du grand jour et de la causerie mais de l'obscurité et du silence."[19] There is of course no basis for believing this resemblance to be evidence of direct influence. Proust, in addition, is emphasizing source, and Virginia Woolf subject. What matters is that long before Virginia Woolf had read Proust,[20] long before Proust had written this passage, there is some evidence of an intellectual sympathy between the two artists, most probably because of their common revolt against positivistic realism.

She had picked up *Cowper's Letters,* the classic prescribed by her father which had bored her, so that one sentence chancing to say something about the smell of broom in his garden, she had thereupon seen the little hall at Richmond laden with flowers on the day of her mother's funeral, smelling so strong that now any flower-scent brought back the sickly horrible sensation; and so from one scene she passed, half-hearing, half-seeing, to another. She saw her Aunt Lucy arranging flowers in the drawing-room.

"Aunt Lucy," she volunteered, "I don't like the smell of broom; it reminds me of funerals."

"Nonsense, Rachel," Aunt Lucy replied.

Here again, not the thought association—such things existed centuries before Virginia Woolf and Proust—but the abrupt and complex transition to which it leads is significant. In an otherwise conventional handling of time, this is a hint of something to come later. These attitudes toward time and personality go back, of course, beyond Proust to Bergson. Such a passage as the following suggests, not the influence of Bergson, but a mind that will be receptive to his concept of reality.

"Does it ever occur to you, Terence [Rachel says], that the world is composed entirely of vast blocks of matter, and that we're nothing but patches of light"—she looked at the soft spots of sun wavering over the carpet and up the wall—"like that?"

But Hewet does not entirely understand; the idea is a fugitive one.

Other fragments of this incipient attitude can be noticed elsewhere in *The Voyage Out.* Terence's picnic party is contrasted with a Sunday-morning Anglican service at the hotel. Terence can take a number of very different individuals and, as a result of his personality, fuse them into a substantial unit: the picnic is a great success. On the other hand, the congregation in the chapel is never unified except mechanically. Time stops during the picnic; the religious service is split into myriad pieces. Anglicanism—formalized Christianity—offers only a sham unity. The church service has an additional significance—as one example of Virginia Woolf's antipathy to religion in this novel. Helen Ambrose says of her children that " 'so far, owing to great care on my part, they think of God as a kind of walrus,' " and she is afraid that someone may teach them the Lord's Prayer during her absence. Helen, Hewet, and Hirst are almost militant non-Christians, and after the church service Rachel joins their ranks. Later, religion—especially organized religion—will become a symbol for Virginia Woolf, but only in her last novel will it be mentioned as often as it is here.

There is also in *The Voyage Out* a hint of what is to become Virginia Woolf's view about "organized society." The "society" of this novel is the hotel and not the London that is left behind. Terence himself has this to say about "organized society":

"Cows ... draw together in a field; ships in a calm; and we're just the same when we've nothing else to do. But why do we do it?—is it to prevent ourselves from seeing to the bottom of things" (he stopped by a stream and began stirring it with his walking-stick and clouding the water with mud), "making cities and mountains and whole universes out of nothing, or do we really love each other, or do we, on the other hand, live in a state of perpetual uncertainty, knowing nothing, leaping from moment to moment as from world to world?—which is, on the whole, the view *I* incline to."

Virginia Woolf's room symbol—apparent in all her work, and especially in *Jacob's Room* and *A Room of One's Own*—has already been noticed in Rachel's tour of the hotel rooms. It appears more explicitly when Rachel says, ironically enough: " 'I hate these divisions. . . . One person all in the dark about another person. . . . Just by going on a ship we cut ourselves off entirely from the rest of the world. I want to see England there—London there—all sorts of people—why shouldn't one? Why should one be shut up all by oneself in a room?' " And another symbol—water—is of primary importance throughout this novel. The water symbol is Virginia Woolf's favorite. Here water is used to suggest life, time, and reality; later it will suggest the three at once. The use of water in this novel is another indication that Virginia Woolf was ready to receive with open arms certain concepts—notably the Bergsonian—soon to become part of the contemporary intellectual climate. Bergson himself often uses water images. Virgina Woolf was denying precisely what Bergson denied; she had chosen water as a symbol for what Lawrence called "the under-life." It would seem only natural, then, that she should have been impressed by echoes of a metaphysic utilizing this same symbol. Having found the metaphysic,[21] she could go on to manipulate her symbol far more rewardingly and more certainly than she used it in *The Voyage Out*.

Despite these tendencies, *The Voyage Out* is in some ways Edwardian. To be sure there is talk of a novel about "silence," but the character who wishes to write this novel—and indeed all the other characters—are perfectly clear-cut; the author is sure of them; the reader is given the illusion of understanding them perfectly; they hold no mysteries except sometimes for each other. But if the characters of this novel are drawn in a pre-eminently Edwardian manner, the emphases and the conclusions are not. There are facts and descriptions, but these are relatively sparse. We do not know what the villa looks like, as we should if Galsworthy had written the novel; we are very rarely told of the style or color of the characters' clothes; we are never certain about what cargo the *Euphrosyne* carries; not until page 90—and then only casually—do we discover why Helen and Ridley Ambrose have gone to South America. It is never quite clear how Terence hopes to support Rachel after their marriage, nor even "what he has." Of course "what one has" is all-important in an Edwardian novel: if it is much, one will probably succeed; if little, one will certainly marry. Just as Henry James generally gave his protagonists money, so that what they did could be explained in terms of themselves rather than of their "situations," so also Virginia Woolf takes for granted the material facts about her people, and concentrates upon motives spiritual and intellectual instead of economic. Like James' and the Russians' novels, *The Voyage Out* is far more concerned with "insides" than with "outsides."

In many ways *The Voyage Out* embodies Leslie Stephen's ideas as to what a novel should do. Stephen died in 1904, just a few years before this novel was written. His obviously powerful personality must have made more than a fleeting impression upon his daughter.[22] But Leslie Stephen's ideas also influenced her:

A novelist is on the border-line between poetry and prose, and novels should be as it were prose saturated with poetry;

a novelist is not only justified in writing so as to prove that his work is fictitious, but he almost necessarily hampers himself, to the prejudice of his work, if he imposes upon himself the condition that his book shall be capable of being mistaken for a genuine narrative;

a novelist professes to describe different actors on his little scene, but he is really setting forth the varying phases of his own mind;

the greatest men [are] dominated by thoughts and emotions which force [those men] to give them external embodiment in life-like symbols.[23]

Stephen believed that novelists should not record the mere fact of day-to-day living (and this is precisely what the Edwardians attempted to do, in imitation of the French naturalists), but rather bring an ideal world to us.[24] Most important, he felt that poetry and philosophy had the same problem—"what is the nature of man and the world in which he lives, and what, in consequence, should be our conduct?"; whereas the philosopher used demonstrations, thought as logic, and direct representation in solving this problem, the artist used intuitions, thought as emotion, and idea represented as symbol.[25]

Virginia Woolf disagreed with some of her father's principles and judgments;[26] but, so far as those mentioned above are concerned, *The Voyage Out* is an example of Stephen's theory.

Leslie Stephen may also be the direct source of one of Virginia Woolf's most interesting themes, barely mentioned in this novel, but on which she was later to play all sorts of variations—the theme of androgyny. As a theme this idea is simple enough: the best men have something of women in them, and the best women something of men. Leslie Stephen wrote in a letter: "Every man ought to be feminine, i.e., to have quick and delicate feelings; but no man ought to be effiminate, i.e., to let his feelings get the better of his intellect and produce a cowardly view of life and the world."[27] In *The Voyage Out* Hewet is complimented by one of the characters as having " 'something of a woman' " in him, and Mrs. Dalloway—who, a good deal changed, is to be the heroine of Virginia Woolf's fourth novel— says of her husband that he " 'gave me all I wanted. He's man and woman as well.' " This is the theme; later developments of it will be extremely complex and significant.

Finally, there is a tendency that, although it later became more conscious and definite, never approached central importance in Virginia Woolf's novels. Several hours after Richard Dalloway terrifies Rachel by beginning to make love to her, she dreams

that she was walking down a long tunnel, which grew so narrow by degrees that she could touch the damp bricks on either side. At length the tunnel opened and became a vault; she found herself trapped in it, bricks meeting her wherever she turned, alone with a little deformed man who squatted on the floor gibbering, with long nails. His face was pitted like the face of an animal. The wall behind him oozed with damp, which collected into drops and slid down. Still and cold as death she lay, not daring to move, until she broke the agony by tossing herself across the bed, and woke crying "Oh!"

Here, it seems, is an author waiting for Freud. But, although Virginia Woolf was one of the first to read Freud, and although the Hogarth Press published English translations of Freud, psychoanalysis seems relatively unimportant in her novels. There are a few passages in which she almost jocularly employs certain

Freudian interpretations, and she is conscious of psychoanalytic techniques, but her novels are never psychoanalytic in any but a general sense of the word. Rachel's dream, for example, is a prophecy of what will happen to her when she falls in love. Although in Freudian terms this dream represents a desire to return to the womb, it probably has no such meaning in the novel. When Rachel's relationship with Terence becomes a fulfillment of the abortive relationship with Richard Dalloway, her dream becomes a reality: the tunnel becomes the Amazon, and especially the path along which she and Terence walk through the jungle; the dampness becomes the humidity of that jungle; the vault becomes the site of her love scene with Terence; the "litttle deformed man" becomes a figure in her delirium; finally, just as in the dream she lay "still and cold as death," so the reality ends for her in death itself.[28]

The Voyage Out may be regarded as a finished work of art, and judged as such. There seems to be no special "struggle" between its form and its content: it accomplishes just what it sets out to accomplish. What can be suggested is that if the tendencies apparent in this novel are developed and crystallized, the result will be a new perspective and—if it is to be successfully communicated in art—a new form. This is, in reality, what happened; certain fleeting ideas of the first novel, given shape and direction by contemporary influences, became central conceptions of later novels. Virginia Woolf's second novel, however, seems to be a new beginning rather than a development insofar as form and thought are concerned; actually, *Night and Day* is the first chapter of Virginia Woolf's artistic development, and *The Voyage Out* the preface.

Night and Day appeared in 1919. It is the longest of Virginia Woolf's novels and, as a comedy of manners, the most conventional in form, tracing the behavior of four principal characters against the social standards of upper-middle-class London. The situation is typical: Katharine Hilbery, granddaughter of the famous English poet Richard Alardyce, has for some time been headed toward marriage with William Rodney in accordance with the social standards of her circle. See accepts him; but then, reacting against her society, she finds another young lady for him to marry, breaks her own engagement, and accepts the lower-middle-class law clerk Ralph Denham, whom, after a series of conventionally complicated circumstances, she finds that she truly loves. Against these characters is set their friend Mary Datchet, a feminist worker whose love for Ralph is finally supplanted by love for her work. Thus the novel ends with three attitudes toward society: Rodney and Cassandra Otway respect it, Mary wishes to reform it, and Katharine and Denham reject it. Since therefore the form of the novel is dependent upon precisely those values the rejection of which for higher values constitutes its theme, there is a serious clash between form and content—between formal and philosophical perspective—which makes *Night and Day* perhaps the least satisfying of Virginia Woolf's novels. It is clearly with Katharine and Denham that the reader is expected to be in league, although their behavior is a norm irreconcilable with the norm of a novel of manners. More important, the form of the novel makes perfectly clear those social values against which hero and heroine rebel, but does nothing to make clear the nature of their higher values, expressed here only most indirectly.

Although it is surely going too far to say that *Night and Day* "might well qualify as the dullest novel in the language,"[29] it is just as surely true that "the novel is a confusion of kinds."[30] Yet it may be supposed that the "failure" of *Night and Day* forced Virginia Woolf to define her perspective, showed her what was essential and what detrimental for its effective communication, and helped her develop its inherent form. "Why ... should there be this perpetual disparity between the thought and the action, between the life of solitude and the life of society, this astonishing precipice on one side of which the soul was active and in broad daylight, on the other side of which it was contemplative and dark as night?" In *The Voyage Out* this problem was ignored: London was left behind at once, and "society"—a society that *could* be reconciled with the individual life—existed as a natural unit. *Night and Day,* on the other hand, is concerned for the most part with the "organized society" of London, whose codes and conventions no longer spring from the individuals who compose it, but rather are superimposed upon them. Here the individual must deny himself if he is to make peace with the dead organism of his society. Society in this sense has stood still as the individual advanced, so that it no longer represents him, no longer suffices to express the body of experience that he has in common with his fellows, or to permit expression of what experience is peculiar to himself. To behave in accordance with society is therefore often to sacrifice truth for "the great make-believe game of English social life."

The symbol for this "truth"—for the higher values—in *Night and Day* is poetry. Thus Katharine's grandfather, one of the truly great poets, was a dismal failure in society. Ralph Denham says that writing poetry is " 'the only thing worth doing,' " and is constantly mistaken for a poet himself although he is a solicitor who has not written poetry since his childhood. Toward the conclusion of the novel, however, "a pulse or stress began to beat at regular intervals in his mind, heaping his thoughts into waves to which words fitted themselves, and without much consciousness of what he was doing, he began to write on a sheet of draft paper what had the appearance of a poem lacking several words in each line. Not many lines had been set down, however, before he threw away his pen as violently as if that were responsible for his misdeeds, and tore the paper into many separate pieces." This because Virginia Woolf is trying to make clear her use of poetry as symbol rather than as fact. For the same reason, Katharine never reads poetry, which she does not like, but spends her leisure time with pure mathematics; Rodney, whose behavior is perfectly conventional, writes dramatic poetry. Cyril Alardyce, who never directly appears in the novel, represents this poetry-society dualism. He, as Katharine's extremely conventional aunt Celia Milvain reminds her, bears the poet's very name, and yet he lives with a common-law wife. Aunt Celia is highly distressed: Cyril must not be unconventional, because he is related to the great poet; actually—in the symbolic sense—this is the very reason for his break with society. In the same way, Katharine and Ralph do not at first wish to marry, since she has repudiated the social order by breaking her engagement to Rodney; finally, however, and unconvincingly, they see marriage as superficial rather than evil as it concerns them.

This symbolism is constant in the novel. After Mr. Hilbery, Katharine's father, has discovered that she has broken her engagement and that Rodney is in love with Cassandra, he tries to use literature as a means of restoring order. He tries to unite the values of poetry and those of society; he fails, even with so mild a thing as a Scott novel:

Civilization had been very profoundly and unpleasantly overthrown that evening; the extent of the ruin was still undetermined; he had lost his temper, a physical disaster not to be matched for the space of ten years or so; and his own condition urgently required soothing and renovating at the hands of the classics. His house was in a state of revolution; he had a vision of unpleasant encounters on the staircase ... was literature itself a specific against such disagreeables? A note of hollowness was in his voice as he read.

Mrs. Hilbery is perfectly able to accept Katharine's change of plans because she believes in poetry. Mrs. Hilbery is a comic character, but her eccentricities have a very serious purpose. She is not introduced as a *divertissement;* on the contrary, her own odd behavior is complementary to Katharine's on the comic level. Mrs. Hilbery's inability to complete her biography of

Richard Alardyce (she writes passage after beautiful passage, but has no plan) is really her refusal to attempt a union of poetry and society. She returns from a pilgrimage to Shakespeare's tomb, and

went on to sing her strange, half-earthly song of dawns and sunsets, of great poets, and the unchanged spirit of noble loving which they had taught, so that nothing changes, and one age is linked with another, and no one dies, and we all meet in spirit, until she appeared oblivious of anyone in the room. But suddenly her remarks seemed to contract the enormously wide circle in which they were soaring and to alight, airily and temporarily, upon matters of more immediate moment.

"Katharine and Ralph," she said, as if to try the sound. "William and Cassandra."

This is a comic echo of the novel's central problem. There is a law, Mrs. Hilbery is able to realize, in poetry that goes below the law of society.

This is a particularly vague way of justifying Katharine's behavior: "something in poetry" is too general to persuade the reader. Virginia Woolf recognized this and, in a significant passage, attempted to justify the mistiness of what Ralph and Katharine call "truth": Katharine

was ready to believe that some people are fortunate enough to reject, accept, resign, or lay down their lives at the bidding of traditional authority; she could envy them; but in her case the questions became phantoms directly she tried seriously to find an answer, which proved that the traditional answer would be of no use to her individually.... The only truth which she could discover was the truth of what she herself felt—a frail beam when compared with the broad illumination shed by the eyes of all the people who are in agreement to see together; but having rejected the visionary voices, she had no choice but to make this her guide through the dark masses which confronted her.... To seek a true feeling among the chaos of the unfeelings or half-feelings of life, to recognize it when found, and to accept the consequences of the discovery.... Much depended, as usual, upon the interpretation of the word love.

In the light of traditional answers, then, Katharine's questions become "phantoms"; but this is no good excuse for the novel's lack of positive values as clear as its negative ones. What this passage does seem to make obvious is that in the framework of a novel of manners Virginia Woolf's perspective must remain a "phantom," just as she herself believed reality to be only a phantom in the framework of the Edwardian novel. The more clearly traditional social values are set forth, the more vaguely higher values can be expressed.

It is well to note at this point that Katharine's "truth" is not an isolated and individual truth, valid for herself alone. She reaches this truth, to be sure, by paying attention to her individual world rather than to the world of society, but when she has found it she can share it with Ralph, with Mrs. Hilbery to a certain extent, with her cousin Henry Otway. If she were to retreat to the individual world, Katharine would be another Rachel Vinrace, and her novel tragedy. In this novel, as in *The Voyage Out,* there recurs the idea that people cannot reach one another—the idea of "the infinite loneliness of human beings." Unlike many of her contemporaries, Virginia Woolf believed that there was a way of overcoming this isolation but that organized society could result in nothing but loneliness for its individual members. When Katharine shows Ralph Denham her mathematical calculations, which she has always hidden between the leaves of a Greek dictionary, and he shows her a scrambled letter he has been writing and an emotional drawing of a dot surrounded with flames, each is for a time embarrassed and ashamed of these halting symbols. But Katharine, looking at Ralph's drawing, says, " 'Yes, the world looks something like that to me, too.' " They begin with inarticulate communication, but Katharine can soon say, " 'You've destroyed my loneliness.' " What prevents communication is simply "the insanely jumbled muddle of a world which impedes the sensible life."

If the "sensible life" is symbolized by poetry, it is also symbolized as a "dream." Katharine and Ralph have "dreams"—daydreams—that seem to them more valid, more to be trusted than much of what really happens to them. So Katharine "fell into a dream state, in which she became another person, and the whole world seemed changed. Being a frequent visitor to that world, she could find her way there unhesitatingly. If she had tried to analyse her impressions, she would have said that there dwelt the realities of the appearances which figure in our world." She recognizes two qualities constant in this dream world: "It was a place where feelings were liberated from the constraint which the real world puts upon them; and the process of awakenment was always marked by resignation and a kind of stoical acceptance of facts." After Denham has met Katharine he recreates her in a dream world, only to fear afterward that "his" Katharine is foreign to the real Katharine; he finds of course that they are the same.

It is feelings that matter in the dream world—impressions as opposed to facts. This is not to say that Virginia Woolf is an impressionist, that she places value on sensation rather than idea. Instead she distrusts the rigidity of fact and thinks more valid the fluidity of impression, as will become clear in her later novels. It is a fact that Cyril Alardyce is living an unconventional, uncivilized life; it is Katharine's impression—she feels—that he is no great scoundrel for doing so. Not to measure one's feelings intellectually, experientially is of course to be simply impressionistic, and in this sense *Night and Day* suffers from an admixture of unsubstantiated feeling with fact. The later novels—those, that is to say, in which form manages to express content—are not impressionistic, but composed of substantiated feeling: feeling proved superior to the apparent fact with which that feeling conflicts. Katharine and Ralph think of themselves as "dreamers" because they have been conditioned to do so by their society; when they challenge that society the illusions become reality, and the society itself an illusion for the most part.

Thus Ralph is afraid that "all his feeling was an illusion." But as soon as he realizes that Katharine too has this "illusion"—that it exists for more than one person and is more than simply an impression—he can see that the "feeling" has led to a reality beneath the surface of society. Ralph and Katharine then accept as real the world of "night," which each had thought the result of isolated caprice, and the novel ends as each whispers " 'Good night' " to the other.

Around this center of "feeling," the main characters of the novel are balanced for an added dramatic effect. Katharine stands for creative and purposeful reason; Rodney, for uncreative reason and adherence of the individual to the social norm; Denham, for creative emotion; and Mrs. Hilbery, for an uncreative emotion that nonetheless allows her to recognize and arrange the catastrophe. Mary Datchet stands, it would seem, for reason denying emotion. Romance—Mrs. Hilbery—is dependent upon Katharine, who searches for fulfillment of herself in dependence upon it. "Splendid as the waters that drop with resounding thunder from high ledges of rock, and plunge downwards into the blue depths of night, was the presence of love she dreamt.... The man, too, was some magnanimous hero, riding a great horse by the shore of the sea." Katharine finds her fulfillment in Denham, and begins to behave like her mother; these eccentricities call from Rodney the comment, " 'Once throw conventions aside ... once do things that people don't do—' and the fact that you are going to meet a young man is no longer proof of anything, except, indeed, that people will talk."

Although Mary Datchet is presented as a sincere and sympathetic character (and clumsily disposed of for that reason), it is worth noting that *Night and Day* is anything but friendly to reform societies in general and feminism in particular. Katharine pictures the feminist workers "murmuring their incantations and concocting their drugs, and flinging their frail spiders' webs over the torrent of life which rushed down the streets outside." Katharine is in favor of the goals of feminism but not of these means for obtaining them. Indeed, Denham thinks of Katharine and Mary that "two women less like each other could scarcely be imagined."

The Voyage Out revealed the seeds of concepts not yet defined in the author's mind. In *Night and Day* Virginia Woolf had more clearly formulated certain of these, but they are more vague here than in the first novel, because they are so at variance with the comedy-of-manners structure into which she attempted to fit them.[31] David Daiches has called *Night and Day* possibly "a novel of ideas masquerading as a social comedy";[32] somewhat more precisely, it could be considered a social comedy pretending to be a novel of ideas, for the "ideas" are hazy when contrasted with the exactitude of form. At any rate, *Night and Day* calls to mind not only certain of the novels of E. M. Forster, but also Virginia Woolf's criticism of Forster's method.

A famous passage from *Howards End* seems more than casually relevant for *Night and Day:* "In public who shall express the unseen adequately? It is private life that holds out the mirror to infinity; personal intercourse, and that alone, that ever hints at a personality beyond our daily vision."[33] Just as Forster's novels oppose country and city—the natural and the unnatural life—so chapters xv–xix, the action of which takes place in and around the county town of Lincoln during the Christmas season, provide a sharp contrast with the rest of *Night and Day*. It is at Lincoln that Ralph sees Katharine for the first time in daylight, and the climax of the novel also occurs here. This symbol is used only fitfully by Virginia Woolf, whereas for Forster it is essential.

In her essay "The Novels of E. M. Forster" Virginia Woolf criticizes what she calls Forster's "double vision":

He sees beauty—none more keenly; but beauty imprisoned in a fortress of brick and mortar whence he must extricate her. Hence he is always constrained to build the cage—society in all its intricacy and triviality—before he can free the prisoner.... Here, then, is a difficult family of gifts to persuade to live in harmony together: satire and sympathy; fantasy and fact; poetry and a prim moral sense. No wonder that we are often aware of contrary currents that run counter to each other.... Yet if there is one gift more essential to a novelist than another it is the power of combination—the single vision. The success of the masterpieces seems to lie not so much in their freedom from faults—indeed we tolerate the grossest errors in them all—but in the immense persuasiveness of a mind which has completely mastered its perspective.

She goes on to say that it is difficult "at once to believe in the complete reality of the suburb and in the complete reality of the soul"; that Forster "has given us an almost photographic picture on one side of the page; on the other he asks us to see the same view transformed and radiant with eternal fires"; and that Forster needs to discover how "to connect the actual thing with the meaning of the thing."[34]

This seems to be a valid statement about Forster's novels; it is certainly a valid statement about *Night and Day*. Virginia Woolf here *shows* the complete reality of the suburb, but asks us to give the greater part of our belief to a soul never made completely real by her. The essay on Forster was written in 1927, the same year in which *To the Lighthouse* appeared, and is therefore interesting in its justification of the form of that novel as well as in its criticism of *Night and Day*.

Forster himself thinks *Night and Day* the least successful of Virginia Woolf's novels.

In view of what preceded it and of what is to follow, *Night and Day* seems to me a deliberate exercise in classicism. It contains all that has characterized English fiction for good or evil during the last hundred and fifty years—faith in personal relations, recourse to humorous side shows, insistence on petty social differences. Even the style has been normalized, and though the machinery is modern, the resultant form is as traditional as *Emma*. Surely the writer is using tools that don't belong to her. At all events she has never touched them again.[35]

Yet it is not so remarkable that Virginia Woolf never used these tools again as that she ever used them at all. In 1919 she not only

wrote *Kew Gardens* and *The Mark on the Wall*—then published
individually and in 1921 together with six other short stories by
the Hogarth Press—but also wrote and published, six months
before the appearance of *Night and Day,* her famous essay "Modern Fiction."[88] The stories, which will be examined later, and
this essay are completely antithetical to the novel, and yet perhaps justify it as an "exercise in classicism" if not as a work of art.

"Modern Fiction" first condemns the Edwardian novelists
Bennett, Wells, and Galsworthy as "materialists," then praises
the kind of thing that Joyce was attempting as "spiritual," and
finally eulogizes the achievements of the Russians.

Galsworthy, Wells, and Bennett—the last-named above all,
because he was the best craftsman of the three—Virginia Woolf
found disappointing despite their technical merits because "they
are concerned not with the spirit but with the body." She calls
them materialists because "they write of unimportant things . . .
they spend immense skill and immense industry making the
trivial and the transitory appear the true and the enduring." (It
can be added that Virginia Woolf commits the same sin by giving so much time to this minor trio.) Their novels have no real
value, because their formal conventionality falsifies life as it is;
their emphases and major concerns are not the emphases and
major concerns of lived life; their probability is the possible
improbable in reality; their plots distort and oversimplify.

Life is not a series of gig lamps, symmetrically arranged; but a
luminous halo, a semi-transparent envelope surrounding us from the
beginning of consciousness to the end. Is it not the task of the novelist
to convey this varying, this unknown and uncircumscribed spirit,
whatever aberration or complexity it may display, with as little mixture of the alien and external as possible? . . . the proper stuff of fiction
is other than custom would have us believe it.

Joyce is the most notable of several new writers, she goes on,
who attempt to "come closer to life" even at the expense of convention, who, unlike some Edwardians, do not confuse means
and end.

Let us record the atoms as they fall upon the mind in the order in which they fall, let us trace the pattern, however disconnected and incoherent in appearance, which each sight or incident scores upon the consciousness. Let us not take it for granted that life exists more fully in what is commonly thought big than in what is commonly thought small.

This celebrated passage, which critics without exception have taken to be an exhortation by Virginia Woolf, is actually nothing of the kind. The very next sentence makes perfectly clear that this passage is a statement, not of Virginia Woolf's intention, but of what she thought to be Joyce's. "Anyone who has read *The Portrait of the Artist as a Young Man* or, what promises to be a far more interesting work, *Ulysses,* now appearing in the *Little Review,* will have hazarded some theory of this nature as to Mr. Joyce's intention." When she goes on to wonder why Joyce, for all his greatness, has not the greatness of Conrad or of Hardy, she decides that this intention and "the comparative poverty of the author's mind" are the reasons, but quickly adds that "any method is right, every method is right, that expresses what we wish to express, if we are writers; that brings us closer to the novelist's intention if we are readers." Method is expression; form and content are one, so that form cannot be thought of or judged by itself in a work of art. Further, the author's own intention is of supreme value, provided it gets expressed as method.

The novelist's problem, she concludes, is "to contrive means of being free to set down what he chooses. He has to have the courage to say that what interests him is no longer 'this' but 'that': out of 'that' alone must he construct his work." She adds that the Russians are writing great novels. But the Russians write Russian novels; the English must write English novels, since the English see and live life differently from the Russians. "The voice of protest is the voice of another and an ancient civilization which seems to have bred in us the instinct to enjoy and fight rather than to suffer and understand." Finally, "nothing—no 'method,' no experiment, even of the wildest—is forbidden, but only falsity and pretense. 'The proper stuff of fiction' does not exist; everything is the proper stuff of fiction, every feeling, every thought; every quality of brain and spirit is drawn upon; no perception comes amiss."

This essay, although denying *Night and Day* as a work of art, justifies it as an "exercise in classicism." In *Night and Day* Virginia Woolf proved for herself the validity of her theory of the novel, and so made valid rather than capricious the necessity for experiment toward a new kind of novel; it is a negative demonstration just as her achieved works of art are positive demonstrations. In this way *Night and Day* is the first step in Virginia Woolf's literary development; the clear definition of "that"—as she uses the word in "Modern Fiction"—was the beginning of a clear definition of "this." So much for the form. Insofar as *Night and Day* fails, insofar as its content is not expressed in its form, it suggests, not only the need for a new formal perspective, but also the need for a regulated philosophical perspective that the formal perspective can articulate as art: there can be no significant form for so vague an artistic ideology as the one that pretends to get itself expressed in this novel. Here the short stories were important: in them the new content was isolated and forced to formalize itself before Virginia Woolf would attempt a sustained formalization. *Jacob's Room,* as a matter of fact, is not that sustained formalization; it complements the short stories; it moves from form to content, just as they move from content to form. The two meet as one for the first time only in *Mrs. Dalloway.*

Virginia Woolf was a radical thinker but a very careful artist—*Night and Day* flows into *Jacob's Room* without any break. Given *Night and Day* and the short stories, the only possible result is *Jacob's Room;* given that, the only possible result is *Mrs. Dalloway. Jacob's Room* is a *modification* of quite conventional form to arrive at new content; the short stories are an *intensification* of new content to express itself through what becomes new form; *Mrs. Dalloway* is a sustained formalization of new content, now regulated. It is the regulation of that content—that philosophical perspective—that must next be considered.

CHAPTER III

THE REGULATION OF A PERSPECTIVE

IRGINIA WOOLF's *Monday or Tuesday,* a book of eight short stories—in a loose sense of that term—was published in 1921. Bernard Blackstone says about it that Virginia Woolf "has her own technique to work out; and these first sketches are *really* sketches."[1] He goes on, as other critics do, to call them "experiments"—attempts, that is, toward writing better novels—suggesting that some of them even seem like sections from longer works. This attitude toward *Monday or Tuesday* seems unsatisfactory. A composer who wished to extend symphonic form would write experimental symphonies and not experimental lieder; in the same way, a novelist—and especially one who had given a great deal of thought to novel form—would probably not think of the short story as part of a novel.

All through her life, Virginia Woolf used at intervals to write short stories. It was her custom, whenever an idea for one occurred to her, to sketch it out in a very rough form and then to put it away in a drawer. Later, if an editor asked her for a short story, and she felt in the mood to write one (which was not frequent), she would take a sketch out of her drawer and rewrite it, sometimes a great many times. Or if she felt, as she often did, while writing a novel that she required to rest her mind by working at something else for a time, she would either write a critical essay or work upon one of her sketches for short stories.[2]

Thus Leonard Woolf makes clear that Virginia Woolf did not write short stories as novel-writing experiments, and that she did not publish her "sketches" until she had reworked them into short stories. The stories in *Monday or Tuesday,* then, were for her neither sketches nor steps toward novels, but fully realized works. Because of this, any extensive examination of them must lie outside the scope of this study. A brief consideration of their philosophical perspective, however, will be helpful.

These stories seem, with the possible exception of "A Society," very strange at a first reading; this is because their form is determined entirely by Virginia Woolf's intention, so that they are not traditional "short stories." They are successful, indeed, to the very extent to which they are not traditional—to the extent, that is, to which their form defines and communicates Virginia Woolf's philosophical perspective as artist, itself "new." The best of them—a short story as completely achieved as the finest of the novels—is perhaps "Kew Gardens."

It is usually said that "Kew Gardens" conveys impression and mood, that it is a postimpressionistic painting in prose.[3] But the story seems actually to be somewhat more than an imitation painting. The reader's attention is focused upon an oval flower bed, and most particularly upon a snail journeying slowly, carefully, assiduously across the flower bed toward some unknown but apparently definite goal. This snail's problems, and his consideration of them, are described with all the care and precision lavished upon a Henry James heroine about to make a moral decision:

> The snail had now considered every possible method of reaching his goal without going round the dead leaf or climbing over it. Let alone the effort needed for climbing a leaf, he was doubtful whether the thin texture which vibrated with such an alarming crackle when touched even by the tip of his horns would bear his weight; and this determined him finally to creep beneath it, for there was a point where the leaf curved high enough from the ground to admit him.

The reader, from the snail's point of view—from the bottom of the flower bed—also watches human passers-by: a husband and wife with their children; two men; two women; a boy with his girl friend. These persons range from very young to very old, from upper- to lower-middle class. And just as the snail is described as a person would usually be, the human beings are described in terms of insects and flowers. "The figures of these men and women straggled past the flower-bed with a curiously irregular movement not unlike that of the white and blue butterflies who crossed the turf in zig-zag flights from bed to bed." "A young man and a young woman ... both in the prime of youth, or even in that season which precedes the prime of youth, the season before the smooth pink folds of the flower have burst their gummy case, when the wings of the butterfly, though fully grown, are motionless in the sun." The humans' conversation drifts over the flower bed as they stop to look down or pass by without noticing; the snail disappears much as Lear's Fool does; everything—persons, flowers, trees, insects—finally dissolves into color by itself, and it "seemed as if all gross and heavy bodies had sunk down in the heat motionless and lay huddled upon the ground, but their voices went wavering from them as if they were flames lolling from the thick waxen bodies of candles." All at once, at the very end of the story, the silence that has been broken only by voices—"wordless voices"—is found not to have been silence at all, for the reader suddenly becomes aware of the noisy, busy city outside the gardens. "Kew Gardens" deserves much more thorough examination than this, but this should suffice for the present purpose.

"Kew Gardens" is a story about "life," in the Bergsonian sense of the word. Briefly—for Bergson's concepts will be used and so made clear in more detail in their relation to the novels—Bergson considers "life" a spiritual force, a vital impetus, equal to "pure" as distinct from chronological time, and equal to human consciousness when that consciousness attains to awareness not measurable by any amount of chronological time (or space)—when, that is, human consciousness attains to holding eternity in an hour, as Blake said. But when life surrenders this attainment or "tension," it becomes mere "extension" or matter. However, there can be no *initiative* until and unless "spirit" (which is pure temporal) outbalances that "matter" (which is spatial, chronological), matter being the noncreative, degenerative action of the vital impetus. Life, therefore, is a battle between freedom (eternity) and necessity (spatial time), for the purpose of inserting as much indetermination (freedom) as possible into matter. There are no "things," there is only this act: life making itself, like an ascending action, and being unmade by extension into matter—materiality—like a descending action. There is this constant movement, flux, transition, duration, which equals "reality." The essence of this movement is one, though many, because the impetus itself is one—there is only one "life itself," one "duration." In short, life is "consciousness launched into matter," that is, *awareness* of the sort that can contain eternity in time (and so is eternal, denying time that must have a stop) *fights to utilize matter,* which is the stuff it has to work through: eternity must be *put* into the hour.

A person cannot "think" eternity—it is not a reasonable entity—and so he must imagine, or intuit, eternity, "life," "pure-time duration." Since Bergsonian reality is unthinkable, unreasonable, it has to be first directly apprehended, then crippled into words. Obviously, if this reality were explicable, it would be thinkable and reasonable. If this explanation were clear, in other words, it would be wrong too.

Since art is imaginative, art can hope to bare reality as technology or philosophy cannot. The artist can re-create, reëstablish the real, in an imaginative *recherche*. What is hopelessly contradictory and smoky (and therefore, according to him, true) in Bergson's philosophy is supremely consistent and translucent in Proust and in Virginia Woolf.

Virginia Woolf worked at second and third hand from the Bergsonism popular enough to permeate the intellectual atmosphere of her age. Because Bergsonism sometimes explains her art—though that art as often helps to explain Bergsonism—it will be useful here; but Virginia Woolf is not to be explained away by one word, "Bergsonism" or any other. Bergsonism is

simply at times a practicable *tool* for the student of Virginia
Woolf, as will become evident a bit later in this study—an ac-
count, let it be remembered, of Virginia Woolf and not at all of
Bergson, of art and not of pure philosophy.

"Kew Gardens" is an attempt to show the "vital impetus" at
work in vegetable, insect, and human life, fighting, with differing degrees of success, the battle against matter. It would be
misinterpretation to say that Virginia Woolf shows a snail to be
more purposeful than a human being, that she sees human
beings merely as insects or vegetables of a sort. The passage contrasting body and voice shows this to be untrue. The "gross and
heavy bodies" are matter; the "thick waxen bodies of candles"
are matter; opposing these are the "voices," the "flames."[5] Certainly the snail is using his part of the vital impetus—or it is
using him—to the utmost; several of the human beings are, on
the other hand, moving toward materiality. This is done not so
much for its irony—although on one level that irony certainly
exists and gives added meaning to the story—as for its emphasis
of the fact that the essence of all this diversity is diversity itself
and hence one: that the duration of the impetus is common,
though in different degrees, to all life—one, not in the mystic's
sense, but in the sense of being manyness itself.

A snail is important in another of these stories, "The Mark on
the Wall," although this sexless, nondramatic snail is a means
rather than an end: it simply provides a stimulus for the narrator's thought. The narrator begins by trying to remember when
she first saw the mark on the wall (the snail, it turns out to have
been). In order to fix the precise date on which she saw it, she
reënacts the entire situation. But the story ends, not with her
giving the date, but with her telling what the mark was. The
facts, in other words, are unimportant; what matters is the
mental play about and from those facts. "The Mark on the
Wall" is a story about a person thinking about thinking about
thinking; it is an exaltation of consciousness. Certainly, if con-

sciousness is considered the *élan vital* in human beings, the free life, it deserves exaltation, for its movement (duration, going on) is time. "I want to think quietly ... never to be interrupted, never to have to rise from my chair ... I want to sink deeper and deeper, away from the surface, with its hard separate facts." So she thinks of innumerable items, one suggesting another, all blending into a whole that is more than the sum of its parts; and she comes back occasionally to the mark on the wall, only to bound further than ever away from it. When her going on is interrupted—when another person enters the room—"everything's moving, falling, slipping, vanishing.... There is a vast upheaval of matter." This reaction agrees perfectly with Bergson: "Our personality descends in the direction of space when the interpenetration of our conscious states becomes broken up and externalized."[6]

"An Unwritten Novel"—another story in which consciousness, using a fact as a jumping-off place, moves creatively—is significant in its burlesque of Freud. The narrator is seated opposite an older woman in a train, and begins to invent a story around her. The woman "twitches"; and the narrator thinks: "Did he [the woman's God] send the itch and the patch and the twitch? Is that why she prays? What she rubs on the window is the stain of sin. Oh, she committed some crime!" This is by far the most amusing story in the book. When facts prove the woman to be a contented mother, and not the miserable spinster created by the narrator: "I'm confounded.... Surely, Minnie, you know better! A strange young man.... Stop! ... I don't know, though. There's something queer in her cloak as it blows." In "The String Quartet" it is music, rather than a fact, that starts the play of consciousness, and the quality of that play is correspondingly different.

Of the other stories, "Monday or Tuesday" and "A Haunted House" are concerned partly with the problem of pure versus chronological time, although this is relatively undeveloped;

"Blue and Green" is an undistinguished prose poem, in which green day and blue night suggest action and thought, whereas "A Society" is a humorous story, only partly successful, of the battle between the sexes, displaying none of the sophistication with which Virginia Woolf was later to handle and resolve this problem.

Although the short stories of *Monday or Tuesday* are short stories and not sketches toward novels, Virginia Woolf's attitudes in some of them are to be found in her later novels as well. The problem of characterization in "An Unwritten Novel" will, for example, be presented on a much higher and more complex plane in *Jacob's Room,* as will certain of the symbols from "Kew Gardens." In addition, the distinction between fact and impression will be found seriously in *To the Lighthouse* and humorously in *Orlando.* This "impression" has nothing to do with impressionism; rather, an impression is the intuitive perception of mobility or reality, whereas a fact is the analytic perception of immobility or appearance—this in Bergsonian terms. The enigma of "An Unwritten Novel"—that is, is what the narrator imagines false because it opposes what she later sees?—is solved when we remember Virginia Woolf's distinction between art and craft in her essay "The Art of Biography":[7] craft is verifiable by fact, whereas art is verifiable by imaginative vision. For Bergson there are two kinds of knowledge: science knows by facts, since it deals with matter in spatial time (science knows matter); philosophy, seeing what it looks upon *sub specie durationis,* knows by pure time. Thus impression is no more subjective than fact, for the vital impetus is common to every living thing (comparable somewhat to Jung's theory of the collective unconscious—the one great dream), and "our knowledge advances by alternate acts of direct acquaintance and analysis."[8] According to this concept, art may be called an analysis of "direct acquaintance" (intuition) which attempts to communicate direct acquaintance. The reader receives the direct acquaintance of art, as the author that of reality, only through analysis. Science and philosophy are not enemies but helpmates. Through analysis of direct acquaintance the artist formalizes direct acquaintance in his work; through analysis of form, the reader apprehends direct acquaintance. The implications of this concept will be seen when *Mrs. Dalloway* is examined.

In *Monday or Tuesday* Virginia Woolf was able to express in short-story form, as art, a perspective conveniently called Bergsonian.° In *Jacob's Room,* despite the adequacy of her philosophical perspective, she was unable to achieve its expression; unlike the content of the stories, the content of the novel did not succeed in finding its proper form, but, like that of *Night and Day,* attempted to express itself through antipathetic formula.

The action of *Night and Day* takes place in eight months, from September until June, and is confined, except for the few chapters set in Lincoln, to London. *Jacob's Room,* a novel one-third as long as *Night and Day,* spans almost a quarter of a century, from about 1891 to about 1915, and its action takes place in England (Cornwall, Scarborough, Cambridge, the Scilly Isles, Essex, London), France, Italy, and Greece. It is divided into fourteen sections, the interval between each indicating a change of time or place; each of these sections is further subdivided as the omniscient narrator moves from one character to another or "interrupts" to say something from her own point of view. This novel has no plot, in the common sense of the term: it tells the story of Jacob Flanders, rather than a story about Jacob Flanders, from his very early childhood until his death, when he is about twenty-seven years old, in the First World War. Jacob is one of the three children, all boys, of Betty Flanders; his father has died two years before the time at which the novel begins. Jacob is taught some Latin by Mr. Floyd, a clergyman friend of his mother; he goes up to Cambridge; he works in a law office in London, reads and thinks a good deal, has numerous love affairs; he spends one of his vacations touring Europe; shortly after the outbreak of the war he is killed in battle. But with these facts Virginia Woolf is not at all concerned. The reader never sees Jacob at his work, never sees him in the war, does not know how or when or where he is killed, for example. The emphases here are almost never where the reader would expect them to be; the "vital statistics" are syncopated, and it is to a group of seemingly trivial incidents in Jacob's life that the reader is directed. The novel, therefore, is not plotless; rather, its plot is its own as an individual novel—or is intended to be.

During the second decade of the twentieth century the "life-novel" was extremely popular. "The life-novel is virtually a new form or mode of writing in England since it is a semi-autobiographic account dealing with a person's life from birth to his discovery of the world. Early influences and the pain of youth are stressed. Generally the central character achieves, in some measure, an understanding of life."[10] Certainly *The Voyage Out* has some affinities with the life-novel; *Jacob's Room,* despite certain superficial resemblances to that novel—both Rachel and Jacob die just when they should be ready to live, for example—has almost nothing in common with the life-novel. The main difference between the two novels is that Rachel can be understood by the reader, whereas Jacob cannot. Rachel thinks, and her thoughts are given the reader—that they are for the most part uninteresting and naïve is not important; she is presented traditionally for what she is; her death, a "vital statistic," is a vital part of the novel. Jacob, on the other hand, is kept distant from the reader, who can never be sure of what he is thinking; his death itself is ignored. Jacob is presented dramatically: his speech, his gestures, his silences are recorded, and the narrator—the most important person in the book—tries, at times, to guess his thoughts on the basis of these externals.

And the Greeks could paint fruit so that birds pecked at it. First you read Xenophon; then Euripides. One day—that was an occasion, by God—what people have said appears to have sense in it; "the Greek spirit"; the Greek this, that, and the other; though it is absurd, by the way, to say that any Greek comes near Shakespeare. The point is, however, that we have been brought up in an illusion.

Jacob, no doubt, thought something in this fashion; the *Daily Mail* crumpled in his hand; his legs extended; the very picture of boredom.

Thus we see Jacob; we hear the narrator attempting, with irrelevant asides, to approximate his thought. But the narrator herself makes clear that it *is* only an attempt: "Nobody sees anyone as he is.... They see a whole—they see all sorts of things—they see themselves." She says twice, in different parts of the book: "It is no use trying to sum people up. One must follow hints, not exactly what is said, nor yet entirely what is done." In accordance with this, conversations are reported only in fragments, and much of "what is done" is syncopated. The narrator is ignorant, not only of Jacob himself, but also of his surroundings. Describing his London flat, she says: "This black wooden box, upon which his name was still legible in white paint, stood between the long windows of the sitting-room. The street ran beneath. No doubt the bedroom was behind"; and she wanders off into an appreciation of eighteenth-century houses. She is embarrassed at her lack of knowledge about Jacob. She tries to dodge the issue by changing the subject; and, accidentally using the word "distinction," she remembers a comment about Jacob and hurries to fill in her own uncertainty with this. The whole description of eighteenth-century rooms, as well as part of a description of Jacob's room at Cambridge, is repeated at the very end of the novel, where the narrator is obviously at a loss for a "summing up." The book ends when Mrs. Flanders, Jacob's mother, wonders what she should do with a pair of his old shoes—the narrator has given up trying.[11] This charming, amusing, and yet profoundly significant attitude of the narrator gives the novel its formal perspective.

J. W. Beach suggests that *Jacob's Room,* "feminine" and "evasive," resembles the manner of Dorothy M. Richardson.[12] This comparison is questionable. Dorothy Richardson tells us, leaving out only those nonverbal bridges symbolized by the dots that sprinkle her pages, precisely what Miriam Henderson is thinking—there can be no doubt that Miriam thinks just what she is said to think. Virginia Woolf's narrator, on the other hand, never tells us what Jacob Flanders is thinking; she tells us only that she cannot tell us, but—"granted ten years' seniority and a difference of sex"—she will do her best at guessing. Jacob's "room"—other people's opinions of him and reactions to him, his gestures, his appearance, his surroundings, his likes and dislikes, some of the things that happen to him—is as close as the narrator can come to Jacob himself. Of course the Edwardian novelists, having given a carefully detailed description and analysis of their characters' "rooms," believed themselves to have done everything. In *Jacob's Room,* the narrator, standing behind Jacob, says that the "room" is only a shadow of Jacob himself; and the author, standing behind the narrator, manipulating the emphases, attempts to show Jacob himself. Virginia Woolf was trying, through a rearrangement of novelistic conventions, to express her own philosophical perspective. *Jacob's Room* is much like *Night and Day,* with the important difference—which makes it a much better novel—that, instead of using traditional formal perspective just as it was, it modifies that perspective in an attempt at compromise between manner and matter. In *Night and Day* convention is used conventionally; in *Jacob's Room,* unconventionally. However, *Jacob's Room* does not seem to be what E. M. Forster has said that it is, Virginia Woolf's "great departure."[13] An examination of the novel's philosophical perspective in relation to its form will make this clear.

Jacob's Room is significantly comparable to *Tom Jones,* which is as a matter of fact Jacob Flanders' favorite novel. Both Fielding and Virginia Woolf's narrator—although in different ways—comment upon their heroes and, in doing so, provide philosophical perspective. Tom Jones very rarely thinks for himself, and has very few opinions: he behaves, and the motives for his behavior are revealed by Fielding rather than by himself. The reader, however, knows what the other characters are thinking, so that it is only Tom who exists in the realm of pure action, thus balancing with Fielding himself, who exists only in the realm of pure thought as commentator. But Fielding's reason for this device is Tom Jones himself: Tom is not reflective, does not think (a shallow exception is his decision to duel, which involves his working out a concept of honor), does not have an interesting mind.

On the other hand, Jacob Flanders is much interested in ideas; what he does, as the emphases of the novel indicate, is not nearly so important as what he thinks; and he has—the reader is given to believe—a most interesting mind. Jacob's own thought and opinion and feeling are what escape the most careful examiner of his "room":

Life is but a procession of shadows, and God knows why it is that we embrace them so eagerly, and see them depart with such anguish, being shadows. And why, if this and much more than this is true, why are we yet surprised in the window corner by a sudden vision that the young man in the chair is of all things in the world the most real, the most solid, the best known to us—why indeed? For the moment after we know nothing about him.

The novel attempts to convey the "sudden vision" of Jacob; yet Jacob's social self is painstakingly built up, and his individual self is only suggested by the narrator's commentary. The reader knows Jacob from all his friends' points of view; he knows what the narrator's own impression of Jacob is; he never knows—and this is the one thing he should know—Jacob himself.

The other characters of the novel think quite conventionally; their thoughts are given directly by an omniscient narrator somewhere behind the immediate narrator. On the first page of the book, for example, Betty Flanders is crying, and looks at the bay before her through tear-filled eyes. Here the reader sees with Mrs. Flanders' eyes and thinks with her mind. Again, the otherwise superb love scene at the Acropolis fails because of this formal conflict: Sandra's thoughts are presented directly whereas Jacob's are approximated by the narrator, who, indeed, goes so far as to conclude the scene with a personal aside that completely demolishes its effect of immediacy.

There are, then, two narrators in charge of *Jacob's Room;* and while one of them is saying that Jacob is essentially unknowable, the other is doing a very good job of disproving that by making the rest of the characters as knowable as they can possibly be. The result is an unresolved disparity in point of view.

No matter which point of view is taken as central it is obvious that, in this novel, form has been superimposed upon content instead of content's being defined by form. If it were possible to see in the narrator immediately present an ironic comment by the author, then *Jacob's Room* might be a completely successful novel. But it is not possible, except perhaps for a subjective reader determined to find order at all cost, as the following passage, in which the immediate narrator appears for the first time, will show.

This astounding agitation and vitality of nature...stirred Betty Flanders and made her think of responsibility and danger. She gripped Archer's hand. On she plodded up the hill.

"What did I ask you to remember?" she said.

"I don't know," said Archer.

"Well, I don't know either," said Betty, humourously and simply, and who shall deny that this blankness of mind, when combined with profusion, mother wit, old wives' tales, haphazard ways, moments of astonishing daring, humour, and sentimentality—who shall deny that in these respects every woman is nicer than any man?

This passage begins from the omniscient narrator's point of view—so that we know what Betty Flanders is thinking—and moves without transition to the point of view of that immediate narrator who will later confess herself unable to say precisely what Jacob is thinking. It would certainly seem that Virginia Woolf had no reason for mixing omniscient point of view with dramatic. *Jacob's Room* is the last of her novels in which she says that it is absolutely impossible for one person to understand another;[14] when, in *Orlando,* she again employed the device of an immediate narrator, she used it with great skill and sureness.

Since the character of Jacob has been conceived and projected by a point of view different from the one that conceived and projected the other characters in the novel, it might seem that any understanding of the philosophical perspective here would be impossible. Are there not *two* interpretations of experience, just as there are two methods of communicating it? But this question supposes *Jacob's Room* to be a completely accomplished work of art, which it is not. Therefore, despite its lack of formal unity, the book has a unity of meaning confused, but not obliterated, by the form that has been imposed upon it. To be sure, this meaning is not adequately expressed through the central character and circumstance of the novel, but it exists in an easily found "residue" beneath character and circumstance. The meaning cannot be dynamic here to any great extent; it is, however, present.

Jacob is first seen as a small child playing upon the beach at Cornwall, where he catches a large sand crab and puts it into his sand bucket. Later, hurried home by his mother because of an oncoming storm, he leaves the bucket on the lawn outside the house in which they are staying during their vacation. Shortly afterward the storm strikes. There are several references by the narrator to this bucket, and to the aster growing near where it stands. Finally: "The rain poured down more directly and powerfully as the wind fell in the early hours of the morning. The aster was beaten to the earth. The child's bucket was half-full of rain-water; and the opal-shelled crab slowly circled round the bottom, trying with its weakly legs to climb the steep

side; trying again and falling back, and trying again and again."
This is, of course, parallel with the situation in "Kew Gardens";
but here the flower is killed and the crab tries in vain to escape
his prison. This too is perfectly consistent with Bergson and
Bergsonistic thinking: the vital impetus does not, in each particular manifestation, win its battle with matter; what is important is that it tries, acts, fights the fight.

This passage concludes the first section of the novel, and therefore has much emphasis given it. The book itself concludes with
Jacob's death in the war: he is fighting the fight against the
materiality of the social structure around him; his own self is
also exhausted and overcome.[15] But the impetus itself is inex-
haustible and not to be overcome.

This makes itself clear in the concluding pages of the novel.
Jacob's friend Bonamy looks about the room in which Jacob will
no longer live.

Bonamy took up a bill for a hunting-crop.
"That seems to be paid," he said.
There were Sandra's letters.
Mrs. Durrant was taking a party to Greenwich.
Lady Rocksbier hoped for the pleasure . . .
Listless is the air in an empty room. . . .
Bonamy crossed to the window. Pickford's van swung down the
street. The omnibuses were locked together at Mudie's corner. Engines
throbbed, and carters, jamming the brakes down, pulled their horses
sharp up. A harsh and unhappy voice cried something unintelligible.
And then suddenly all the leaves seemed to raise themselves.
"Jacob! Jacob!" cried Bonamy, standing by the window. The leaves
sank down again.
"Such confusion everywhere!" exclaimed Betty Flanders, bursting
open the bedroom door.
Bonamy turned away from the window.
"What am I to do with these, Mr. Bonamy?"
She held out a pair of Jacob's old shoes.

Jacob's "room" is gone; of that there can be no doubt. But
Bonamy goes to the window; the noise and the struggle of life

going on outside lead him to call out the name of his friend.
Jacob himself—the essential Jacob—is still alive in the confusion
and the flux of life itself. Mrs. Flanders, unable to apprehend
this, complains of the "confusion." She is, ironically, unhappy
that she cannot reduce this vital disorder to a material order;
when Bonamy turns back from the window, she is holding the
shoes, as though to understand Jacob's "room" would be to understand Jacob himself. But unfortunately the room is all of
Jacob that Virginia Woolf demonstrably presents in this novel.
The form of this novel is inadequate to express Jacob himself—
what the author feels to be the reality of the individual. Yet the
reader comes much closer to that reality here than he was able to
do in *Night and Day*.

The body-voice, candle-flame contrasts of "Kew Gardens" also
reappear in *Jacob's Room*. Thus, for example: "The voice had an
extraordinary sadness. Pure from all body." "The beauty of
women ... is like the light on the sea, never constant to a single
wave.... Now she is dull and thick as bacon; now transparent
as a hanging glass." These images serve to underline the difference between "room" and essence, as do countless others
throughout the novel.

If human character is not what it seems—if it is not definable
in terms of its "room"—neither is time.[16] *Jacob's Room* is the
first of Virginia Woolf's novels to reflect the new Bergsonian
concept of time. Real time is mobility; clock time is immobility.
After cataloguing a number of facts, the narrator of *Jacob's
Room* says: "Spaces of complete immobility separated each of
these movements.... The worn voices of clocks repeated the fact
of the hour all night long." The disparity between clock time and
reality is shown at length in another passage later in the book:

The clock struck the quarter.
  The frail waves of sound broke among the stiff gorse and the
hawthorn twigs as the church clock divided time into quarters.
  Motionless and broad-backed the moors received the statement "It

is fifteen minutes past the hour," but made no answer, unless a bramble stirred....

Often, even at night, the church seems full of people.... Their tongues join together in syllabling the sharp-cut words, which for ever slice asunder time and the broad-backed moors....

At midnight when no one speaks or gallops, and the thorn tree is perfectly still, it would be foolish to vex the moor with questions— what? and why?

The church clock, however, strikes twelve.

The union of church and clock time is significant: both, Virginia Woolf felt, were false orders—methods superimposed upon life rather than justified by the nature of life itself.[17]

Organized society too is an imposition, and a fatal one. At the opera house, "to prevent us from being submerged by chaos, nature and society between them have arranged a system of classification which is simplicity itself; stalls, boxes, amphitheatre, gallery.... But the difficulty remains—one has to choose.... Never was there a harsher necessity! or one which entails greater pain, more certain disaster; for wherever I seat myself, I die in exile: Whitaker in his lodging-house; a Lady Charles at the manor." The "chaos," like Betty Flanders' "confusion," is mobile reality; the "system" is sham; the "room" is appearance. "The overpowering sorrow ... we start transparent, and then the cloud thickens. All history backs our pane of glass. To escape is vain." This last is a guess at Jacob's thought, but "whether this is the right interpretation of Jacob's gloom ... it is impossible to say." Clara Durrant, who, although she is in love with Jacob, will never allow him to say any more than convention allows, typifies the individual who permits himself to be molded entirely by his society. Clara is a composite of the young Rachel Vinrace and the young Katharine Hilbery; she plays Bach and pours tea eternally; she is "a virgin chained to a rock (somewhere off Lowndes Square)." And the working-class formula, though usually not self-imposed, is shown to be no better than Clara's.

Virginia Woolf reveals, in a brief sketch of Jinny Carslake's "philosophy," that the unity she has attempted to communicate in this novel is no traditional unity beneath multiplicity.

[Jinny], after her affair with Lefanu, the American painter, frequented Indian philosophers, and now you find her in pensions in Italy cherishing a little jeweller's box containing ordinary pebbles picked off the road. But if you look at them steadily, she says, multiplicity becomes unity, which is somehow the secret of life, though it does not prevent her from following the macaroni as it goes round the table, and sometimes, on spring nights, she makes the strangest confidences to shy young Englishmen.

Sandra's platitudes are treated in the same way, and Jacob's own metaphysical entanglements the narrator views with respect for their sincerity but with patient amusement for their futility. It is clearly not a quantitative unity that Virginia Woolf envisions. Rather, like Bergson, she presents a qualitative multiplicity—the oneness of manyness.

Twice during the course of this novel the meaning ceases to be only residual and becomes to a certain extent dynamic—that is, in two extended passages the content of *Jacob's Room* is quite adequately achieved as form. The first of these passages is the beginning section of the book, where nervous shifts from one person to another not only emphasize the personality of Mrs. Flanders and create for the reader a suitable response to the hurricane that occurs in the section, but also express the impetus that unifies human and nonhuman life. The reader jumps from Mrs. Flanders' point of view to Archer's, to Charles Steele's, to the immediate narrator's and Jacob, back to Mrs. Flanders', and finally to a description of the storm in which a spotlight is turned now upon the sleeping Jacob, now upon the sky, now upon the aster and crab that fight a losing battle for survival. The points of view are diverse, but the focus is always upon a common energy, so that the reader is made aware of an essential rather than a merely superficial diversity—a qualitative diversity beneath the quantitative diversity.

Again, the transition technique employed in the thirteenth section of the novel—a technique that is to be important in *Mrs. Dalloway*—accomplishes the meaning in its emphasis of simultaneity rather than succession and of a heterogeneous rather than a homogeneous time. The reader sees a runaway horse from the point of view of Clara and Mr. Bowley; time is shifted forward an hour; then the reader is snapped back again to the horse, this time from Julia Eliot's point of view. Julia remembers that she must be at Lady Congreve's at five o'clock. Time now provides a transition: Florinda sees a clock striking five. She remarks that someone whom she has noticed resembles Jacob, and the reader moves to where Jacob is seated in Hyde Park. Jacob reads a letter from Sandra Wentworth Williams, and the reader moves to her. Sandra is thinking of Jacob, and the reader returns to him. Jacob talks to a ticket collector, making possible a transition to Fanny Elmer, who, walking on the Strand, is thinking of Jacob's manner of talking to such people. Fanny boards a bus, which passes Westminster as Big Ben strikes five o'clock. To be sure, there is no absolute negation of clock time here, as there is in *Mrs. Dalloway,* nor is the device used here with the mastery that makes it so successful in that novel; but it does afford an illustration of one means by which Virginia Woolf was later able to accomplish her end, and even here it does spring from—rather than superimpose itself upon—the content.

A serious flaw, characterizing not only these sections but also *Jacob's Room* as a whole, does result from the inexpert use of this device. Although these rapid transitions succeed to a large extent in communicating the book's meaning, they have the more immediate effect of making *Jacob's Room* seem incoherent, especially since it is already handicapped by having two conflicting narrators. In her diary Virginia Woolf speaks of *Jacob's Room* as "spasmodic,"[18] which would indicate that she herself recognized this flaw.

The "room" concept is pervasive in Virginia Woolf's writing. It first appears in Rachel Vinrace's tour of hotel rooms in *The Voyage Out* and elsewhere in that novel. It is less emphasized, but still important, in *Night and Day,* where the little room in which Richard Alardyce's effects are exhibited is a good illustration of the concept. In *Mrs. Dalloway* and *To the Lighthouse* it is quite important, and it can be found in all the remaining novels. In Virginia Woolf's nonfiction the "room" concept is especially evident in "A Letter to a Young Poet" and of course in *A Room of One's Own.* Some critics have attempted general explanations of this concept. Thus Ruth Gruber believes that Virginia Woolf saw in all her work the room as reality and the view outside the window as illusion.[19] John Graham says that the room often symbolizes "the selfhood formed in time," and that the window always symbolizes "the outlook of the self on the world around it."[20]

Such explanations, although they are interesting, are not completely satisfying, since it seems obvious that Virginia Woolf used room-window symbolism in no one restricted sense but rather in accordance with the all-over significance of each work in which it appears. For example, when in "A Letter to a Young Poet"[21] she advises the poet to look out of the window for his material, she is telling him, not to base his work upon illusion rather than reality, but simply to be objective. On the other hand, the "room" in *Jacob's Room* is neither reality nor "the selfhood formed in time," but the illusory social self. Further, to read the last scene of *Jacob's Room* as one in which the window symbolized "the outlook of the self on the world around it" would be virtually impossible: it is Bonamy who looks from Jacob's window here, and he sees Jacob outside the room.

It would seem, then, that there is no consistent usage of this symbol. In *Jacob's Room,* for example, the room is the social self;

in "A Letter to a Young Poet" it is the individual self. The symbolism of the room can best be understood, not in itself, but in its context in each work. It is possible to generalize only to the extent of being aware that the concept behind this kind of symbol supposes a distinction—perfectly obvious, of course— between a person's appearance and his real nature, or, to use the language of "Modern Fiction," between the "material" and the "spiritual." Spirit cannot be expressed or grasped in terms of matter alone, which is not only a falsification but actually a nega- tion of spirit. Reduced to its maximum generality, this concept is representable by Bergson's space-time, determination-freedom, environmental-self–becoming-self antithesis.

It was this "spirit" that *Jacob's Room* insisted to be reality but was unable convincingly to communicate. In her next novel, however, Virginia Woolf did succeed in communication of what she believed to be reality. She succeeded because, instead of using accepted form and attempting a compromise between it and her subject matter, she allowed the subject matter to de- termine its form. But it may be suggested that the basis of her success in *Mrs. Dalloway* was her realization of the importance of *memory* to her vision of life: Mrs. Dalloway remembers, and, by communicating her remembrance, Virginia Woolf is able to communicate her "spirit" as well as her "room."

Mrs. Dalloway was published in 1925. In a special introduc- tion she wrote in 1928 for the Modern Library edition of this novel, Virginia Woolf said some very significant things about its genesis:

The book, it was said, was the deliberate offspring of a method. The author, it was said, dissatisfied with the form of fiction then in vogue, was determined to beg, borrow, steal or even create another of her own. But, as far as it is possible to be honest about the mysterious process of the mind, the facts are otherwise. Dissatisfied the writer may have been; but her dissatisfaction was primarily with nature for giving an idea, without providing a house for it to live in. The novelists of the preceding generation had done little—after all why should they?—to help. The novel was the obvious lodging, but the novel it seemed was built on the wrong plan. Thus rebuked the idea started as the oyster starts or the snail to secrete a house for itself. And this it did without any conscious direction. The little notebook in which an attempt was made to forecast a plan was soon abandoned, and the book grew day by day, week by week, without any plan at all, except that which was dictated each morning in the act of writing. The other way, to make a house and then inhabit it, to develop a theory and then apply it, as Wordsworth did and Coleridge, is, it need not be said, equally good and much more philosophic. But in the present case it was necessary to write the book first and to invent a theory afterwards.

The result was a novel printed, except for a few double spaces between paragraphs, as an undivided unit. The immediate scene is London, and the immediate time a Wednesday in the middle of June, 1923. The story is simply a description of this day as it was lived by Clarissa Dalloway, her husband, her friend Peter Walsh, Septimus Warren Smith (an insane man whom she does not know or meet), and several other people of lesser importance. Clarissa herself, socially prominent because her husband is a Member of Parliament (Conservative), is fifty-two years old, lives in Westminster, and has a daughter of seventeen. Although Clarissa is the daughter of a country parson, she has become a social butterfly who takes great delight in giving large and successful parties: she is a perfect hostess. There is a Clarissa Dalloway in *The Voyage Out,* of course, but she bears little resemblance to this Clarissa. As Winifred Holtby has said, Clarissa in *The Voyage Out* is a peer's daughter who plays the piano and lives in Mayfair.[22] The facts about the two Clarissas are different, and there is in the earlier only a hint of the later.[23]

Mrs. Dalloway is not primarily about Clarissa, or about any of its other characters. Rather, it is about life and reality or time; both character and circumstance are means to the end of expressing a unified vision of experience. Just as, in "Mr. Bennett and Mrs. Brown," Virginia Woolf had defined Mrs. Brown as "the spirit we live by, life itself," so in *Mrs. Dalloway* emphasis is placed not so much upon Mrs. Dalloway the individual person as upon Mrs. Dalloway's ability to mirror "life itself": she is what might be called a carrier of life. This life or "spirit" is communicated, not by means of Mrs. Dalloway's "room," but by her consciousness.

Bergson had defined life as "consciousness launched into matter." *Mrs. Dalloway* represents the conflict, not between person and person, but between duration and false time. On twenty occasions during the course of the novel, clocks strike—"shredding and slicing, dividing and subdividing, the clocks ... nibbled at the June day, counselled submission, upheld authority, and pointed out in chorus the advantages of a sense of proportion"—and against the materiality of this spatialized day in London is placed the spirituality, the true duration, of Mrs. Dalloway's consciousness, the continuity of which denies that "dividing and subdividing." Mrs. Dalloway refuses to separate herself as an individual from the rest of the world. "She felt herself everywhere; not 'here, here, here'; and she tapped the back of the seat; but everywhere. She waved her hand, going up Shaftesbury Avenue. She was all that." "She would not say of any one in the world now that they were this or were that ... to her it was absolutely absorbing; all this; the cabs passing; and she would not say of Peter, she would not say of herself, I am this, I am that." Clarissa will not circumscribe herself, separate herself from anyone or anything else.

There are two villains in this novel: the goddesses of proportion and conversion. In the distinguished psychiatrist Sir William Bradshaw is enshrined "proportion, divine proportion, Sir William's goddess." Sir William is also a worshipper at the shrine of conversion, but it is the pathetic Doris Kilman in whom conversion lives most obviously. The crime these goddesses commit is destruction of freedom by enforcement of obedience to an artificial society. Sir William sets himself up as judge of what is madness, what sense; Miss Kilman of what is evil, what good. Having decided, they proceed to correct whatever wanders from their personal conception of normality: it is conversion who "feasts on the wills of the weakly, loving to impress, to impose, adoring her own features stamped on the face of the populace"; who "bestows her blessing on those who, looking upward, catch submissively from her eyes the light of their own."

Just as this greatest crime is an imposition of the self and its standards upon others, so the greatest virtue is surrender of the self, not to its own or another's arbitrary rule, but to what Bergson would call the spirit or supraconsciousness—memory: pure-time existence or duration. It is this surrender that Clarissa and Septimus, each on a different level, are finally able to accomplish—this that constitutes the real movement of the novel. For the morning-to-evening movement is set up as a false, a spatial movement; opposed to it is the true movement of reality.

This becomes perfectly clear when the relationship between Clarissa and Septimus is considered. Virginia Woolf says: "In the first version Septimus, who later is intended to be [Mrs. Dalloway's] double, had no existence...Mrs. Dalloway was originally to kill herself, or perhaps merely to die at the end of the party."[24] In either event there would have been the breaking down of the wall between self and not-self that is the novel's affirmation; but the novel as it stands is much more satisfying than it would have been if this had occurred only on the physical level. Both Septimus and Mrs. Dalloway are insane—he actually, she in a metaphorical sense—for neither will accept the "sanity" around them as real. Both Septimus and Mrs. Dalloway have therefore to find a way of escaping from the false life to what they believe true reality. Septimus, a victim of shock in the war, does this by defying his doctors and leaping from a window to his death, and Clarissa by annihilating her individuality (and thus killing her self—gaining true individuality).

Septimus does not wish to die when he commits suicide; he dies, not to escape life, but to escape death in life. In his insanity, like one of Shakespeare's "wise fools," he speaks truth. He thinks: "Leaves were alive; trees were alive. And the leaves being connected by millions of fibres with his own body, there on the seat, fanned it up and down; when the branch stretched he, too, made that statement"; and he moans that he suffers from "eternal loneliness,"and mutters that "communication is health; communication is happiness." He is thus echoing Clariassa's belief that "she was all that." It is his love of life, his belief in unity, then, that Septimus affirms by casting away his physical individuality.

Throughout the novel, Clarissa has been moving toward the same self-effacement. When, at her party, she hears of the young man's suicide, she retires to a little room and empathetically experiences Septimus' death. Then suddenly she realizes their affinity."A thing there was that mattered; a thing, wreathed about with chatter, defaced, obscured in her own life, let drop every day in corruption, lies, chatter. This he had preserved. Death was defiance. Death was an attempt to communicate; people feeling the impossibility of reaching the centre which, mystically, evaded them; closeness drew apart; rapture faded, one was alone. There was an embrace in death." She thinks, as she has thought before: "If it were now to die, 'twere now to be most happy." In the light of her whole past life, which has been recaptured by her during the day, she goes on, having criticized herself, to realize that "no pleasure could equal . . . this having done with the triumphs of youth, lost herself in the process of living."

The clock began striking. The young man had killed himself; but she did not pity him; with the clock striking the hour, one, two, three, she did not pity him, with all this going on. . . . the words came to her, Fear no more the heat of the sun.... She felt somehow very like him—the young man who had killed himself. She felt glad that he had done it; thrown it away. The clock was striking. The leaden circles dissolved in the air. He made her feel the beauty; made her feel the fun.... And she came in from the little room.

John Graham, in a distinguished essay, writes that when Clarissa "leaves the little room she returns to the larger room of human relations" and symbolizes time's transfiguration by eternity. Thus far he seems to have the correct interpretation. But when he adds that "we must retain the limiting, protecting identity which is ours in time if we are to triumph over time," it becomes probable that his interpretation is not a description of what really happens in the novel.[25] Clarissa has come in from the little room of her own identity to the large room of reality itself. It is made explicit that her party is much more than a social gathering—and so her entrance more than the assumption of a social identity: her parties are an "offering." Nor, as the little-room scene makes just as explicit, does Clarissa retain her individual identity; rather it is a case of "not I, but Time in me." Clarissa has in a strict sense found her life by losing it.

Clarissa is constantly afraid of losing her life. She is not yet completely recovered from a recent illness; she is more than a little jealous when her husband goes by himself to lunch with Lady Bruton; above all, she is aware of growing old, of being old. "She feared time itself, and read on Lady Bruton's face, as if it had been a dial cut in impassive stone, the dwindling of life; how year by year her share was sliced; how little the margin that remained was capable any longer of stretching, of absorbing, as in the youthful years, the colours, salts, tones of existence, so that she filled the room she entered, and felt often...an exquisite suspense, such as might stay a diver before plunging." This fear of time—of false time—runs through the book. Beginning the day, Clarissa glances into Hatchards' window and sees a book lying open there. "Fear no more the heat o' the

sun / Nor the furious winter's rages," she reads. The phrase
"Fear no more" recurs four times in the novel, three times to
Clarissa and once in Septimus' thought; although its first appearance is ironic—Clarissa *does* fear—the phrase gathers new
and increased meaning with each use, and comes finally to have
its literal meaning for her.

This is not to say that Clarissa comes unaware to her final
affirmation; even at the beginning of the novel, she has within
her all the potentialities that are to become actualities.

She remembered once throwing a shilling into the Serpentine. But
everyone remembered; what she loved was this, here, now, in front
of her.... somehow in the streets of London, on the ebb and flow of
things, here, there, she survived, Peter survived, lived in each other,
she being part, she was positive, of the trees at home ... of people she
had never met; being laid out like a mist between the people she
knew best, who lifted her on their branches as she had seen the trees
lift the mist, but it spread ever so far, her life, herself.

This undervaluation of remembrance is ironic, for it is precisely
remembrance that will enable Clarissa to refind her past and
apprehend duration. The return of Peter Walsh from India, and
his sudden visit to her, cause a rush of time past into the present
moment; the resulting simultaneity destroys clock time and
Clarissa's fear of clock time.

If Septimus is Clarissa's double, Peter Walsh is her opposite.
For one moment he does escape time. "He had escaped! was
utterly free—as happens in the downfall of habit when the
mind, like an unguarded flame, bows and bends and seems about
to blow from its holding. I haven't felt so young for years!
thought Peter, escaping (only of course for an hour or so) from
being precisely what he was." Peter is perhaps meant to represent the average person: he can escape time for a little while, but
will not allow himself to be free for good, so greedily does he
hold on to "precisely what he is." Thus Peter has the habit of
fidgeting with a pocketknife, and in one scene the meaning of

this habit is made explicit. "The brain must wake now. The body must contract now, entering the house, the lighted house, where the door stood open, where the motor cars were standing, and bright women descending: the soul must brave itself to endure. He opened the big blade of his pocket-knife." Simply, Peter protects his individuality from society and refuses to surrender it; yet, in so doing, he is giving himself up to the society that he fears. As the ambulance bears Septimus' dead body away Peter watches it pass, and thinks that it is a symbol of the triumph of civilization—"the efficiency, the organization, the communal spirit of London"—whereas it is actually a symbol of the hated goddesses of proportion and conversion.

The transitional device used in *Jacob's Room* in the runaway-horse sequence appears, much more successfully, in *Mrs. Dalloway*. The limousine that bears some royal personage—"Queen, Prince, or Prime Minister nobody knew"—moves slowly to the palace, and the reader sees it now from one point of view, now from another: it accomplishes in its progress the idea of spatialization. But those who wait outside the palace gates to see it enter forget about it when an airplane begins to skywrite. The limousine passes unnoticed, each onlooker straining to make out the letters of white smoke forming against the sky. "As they looked the whole world became perfectly silent, and a flight of gulls crossed the sky, first one gull leading, then another, and in this extraordinary silence and peace, in this pallor, in this purity, bells struck eleven times, the sound fading up there among the gulls." Here spatialization is contrasted with simultaneity. The main conflict of the novel is thus set up at the outset. David Daiches is unconvincing when he says: "Whenever a clock strikes in *Mrs. Dalloway* it is because the author is going to move from one character to others, and is emphasizing the moment of time in virtue of which these disparate individuals are related."[29] Clock time is not always used as a transition; nor are individuals ever unified by clock time. When persons are shown as diverse in the same moment of clock time, it is rather the false unity of clock time that is being illustrated. Not clock time, but mobile true time—"that divine vitality which Clarissa loved," "a match burning in a crocus"—is unity.

Virginia Woolf's concept of this unity has determined the techniques of characterization in *Mrs. Dalloway*. The main characters here are not to be summed up in a phrase; neither have they the almost tangible immediacy of Eliot's Grandcourt, of Conrad's Razumov, or of the characters in Virginia Woolf's own early novels. In *La Prisonnière* Proust asked:

Et, en elles-mêmes, qu'étaient Albertine et Andrée? Pour le savoir, il faudrait vous immobiliser, ne plus vivre dans cette attente perpétuelle de vous où vous passez toujours autres, il faudrait ne plus vous aimer, pour vous fixer, ne plus connaître votre interminable et toujours déconcertante arrivée. ... du faux jugement de l'intelligence, laquelle n'entre en jeu que quand on cesse de s'intéresser, sortiront définis des caractères stables de jeunes filles, lesquels ne nous apprendront pas plus que les surprenants visages apparus chaque jour quand, dans la vitesse étourdissante de notre attente, nos amies se présentaient tous les jours, toutes les semaines, trop différentes pour nous permettre, la course ne s'arrêtant pas, de classer, de donner des rangs.[27]

For the same reason Mrs. Dalloway "would not say of herself, I am this, I am that"; and, if not of herself, then not of Peter or anyone else either. Dr. Holmes and Sir William Bradshaw are only too willing to immobilize, to classify human beings; this is their great error. For a reason closely akin to Proust's, Mrs. Brown is defined as "life itself." If the characters here were sharply defined, the techniques of the novel would be going contrary to its meaning rather than expressing that meaning. Instead, "life itself"—a vision of life that denies the validity of boundaries—must be projected through the characters.

It is evidently not a flaw, as Philip Toynbee considers it, that "there has been a failure of differentiation" in *Mrs. Dalloway* since the "same atmosphere and language enclose nearly all the people in this book."[28] Virginia Woolf's people think in the same language, precisely because she is insisting that there can be no differentiation in reality. The oneness of language is the oneness of the vital impetus beneath diversity.[29]

That Virginia Woolf had read and learned from Proust is evident not only in the characterization of *Mrs. Dalloway,* but also in a Proustian use of metaphor that does much to give this novel its total effect. In her series of articles on "Phases of Fiction" in the *Bookman,* Virginia Woolf said that, through his use of metaphor, Proust had been able to achieve poetic effects in his novel: he was able to rise above the specific details to a generalization about all of experience, and at the same time to give the details themselves symbolic value.[30] She herself put this device to use again and again in *Mrs. Dalloway:*

"For you should see the Milan gardens," she said aloud. But to whom?

There was nobody. Her words faded. So a rocket fades. Its sparks, having grazed their way into the night, surrender to it, dark descends, pours over the outlines of houses and towers; bleak hillsides soften and fall in. But though they are gone, the night is full of them; robbed of colour, blank of windows, they exist more ponderously, give out what the frank daylight fails to transmit—the trouble and suspense of things conglomerated there in the darkness; huddle together in the darkness; reft of the relief which dawn brings when, washing the walls white and grey, spotting each window-pane, lifting the mist from the fields, showing the red-brown cows peacefully grazing, all is once more decked out to the eye; exists again. I am alone; I am alone! she cried.[31]

Here Rezia's thought moves from the specific to the general, and the resulting simile serves to give her state of mind significance in terms of the vision of life conveyed by the novel as a whole. In such passages as this—and it is almost impossible to say if the simile belongs to Rezia or to the central intelligence of the book—an immediate experience is clarified by the total meaning of the novel at the same time as that meaning is clarified by the experience.

A more complex and extensive use of such metaphor occurs toward the end of the novel; the entire party sequence is given meaning, and the meaning itself made dynamic, through the implications of the figure here. Clarissa is leading the prime minister through the room. "She wore ear-rings, and a silver-green mermaid's dress. Lolloping on the waves and braiding her tresses she seemed, having that gift still; to be; to exist; to sum it all up in the moment as she paused; turned . . . laughed, all with the most perfect ease and air of a creature floating in its element. But age had brushed her; even as a mermaid might behold in her glass the setting sun on some very clear evening over the waves." The water image has appeared throughout the novel to symbolize unity; Bergson said: "The unity of the impulse which, passing through generations, links individuals with individuals, species with species, and makes of the whole series of the living one single immense wave flowing over matter."[82] Clarissa is above the waves, but Peter thinks that she "must now, being on the very verge and rim of things, take her leave." And she does. Going off into the little room, she thinks of Septimus' leap from the window. "Had he plunged holding his treasure?" His act, then, was a plunge, the same kind of plunge with which the novel began—"What a lark! What a plunge! For so it had always seemed to her, when . . . she had burst open the French windows and plunged at Bourton into the open air. . . . the air was . . . like the flap of a wave; the kiss of a wave." Again throughout the novel the appearance, the matter, of clock time has been denied by true time in an air-water metaphor often repeated: Big Ben strikes, and "the leaden circles dissolved in the air." There follows, in the little room, Clarissa's rich identification with Septimus and her own plunge, dissolution, annihilation.

The certainty with which Virginia Woolf used metaphor in *Mrs. Dalloway* should be sufficient indication that she "imitated" Proust only in the best sense of the word. Her early novels show that what she found in Proust was largely a confirmation of ideas she had already began to work out for herself, and—more important—proof that such ideas could be rendered into great art. It is natural that Proust appealed to Virginia Woolf; her own concerns, her own terms—impressions, facts, reality, time—were his. Proust's definition of "reality" in *Le Temps retrouvé*—"Tout simplement notre vie, la vraie vie, la vie enfin découverte et éclaircie, la seule vie par conséquent réellement vécue, cette vie qui en un sens, habite à chaque instant chez tous les hommes aussi bien que chez l'artiste"—is Virginia Woolf's; it is "life itself." Proust continues:

Mais ils ne le voient pas, parce qu'ils ne cherchent pas à l'éclaircir ... Ressaisir notre vie; et aussi la vie des autres; car le style pour l'écrivain aussi bien que pour le peintre est une question non de technique, mais de vision. Il est la révélation qui serait impossible par des moyens directs et conscients de la différence qualitative qu'il y a dans la façon dont nous apparaît le monde, différence qui, s'il n'y avait pas l'art, resterait le secret éternel de chacun.[33]

In perfect agreement, Virginia Woolf says of reality:

Whatever it touches, it fixes and makes permanent.... that is what is left of past time and of our loves and hates. Now the writer, as I think, has the chance to live more than other people in the presence of this reality. It is his business to find it and collect it and communicate it to the rest of us. So at least I infer from reading *Lear* or *Emma* or *La Recherche du Temps Perdu*.... one sees more intensely afterwards; the world seems bared of its covering and given an intenser life.[34]

"A writer should give us direct certainty."[35] "The reality which our poets and novelists have to expound and illuminate,"[36] if they are to re-create the other world of which people are "mysteriously a part without knowing it,"[37] will be embodied in an artistic masterpiece only when "the vision is clear and order has been achieved."[38] To be sure, Virginia Woolf does not minimize the importance of "technique," but she does insist that the "vision" has primary importance and that technique must achieve the vision and be the vision as art; so technique cannot possibly precede the vision. The very movement of *Mrs. Dalloway* is Clarissa's "recherche du temps perdu" and final synthesis of past and present, brought about largely by Peter Walsh's sudden return and Septimus' death. It will be seen that Proust's novel is often a valuable commentary upon Virginia Woolf's later work as well, where she seems occasionally to have developed, in her own way, themes suggested by him.[39] Indeed, if many of Virginia Woolf's concepts are most satisfactorily representable in Bergsonistic terms, it is Proust—and not Bergson himself or anyone else—who offered the most important single contribution to her work. Her later novels reach conclusions about life and experience not at all dependent upon Bergsonism for their validity.

Many critics have, although for the most part ignoring the relation of Proust's art to *Mrs. Dalloway,* declared that the book was profoundly influenced by James Joyce, especially by *Ulysses.* For example, J. Isaacs calls it an "inspired imitation of *Ulysses,*"[40] and A. R. Reade thinks it possibly a criticism of *Ulysses.*[41] The two reasons why most critics see such an influence are that both *Mrs. Dalloway* and *Ulysses* take place on one day, and that both, supposedly, employ the "stream of consciousness" method.

Just as Virginia Woolf explicitly admired *À la Recherche du temps perdu,* she explicitly disliked *Ulysses.* It has already been mentioned that she spoke of Joyce's "comparative poverty of mind"; she described *Ulysses* as "a memorable catastrophe—immense in daring, terrific in disaster."[42] It is doubtful that she would have wished to imitate a novel about which she had such an opinion. Certainly she admired Joyce's attempt; certainly she approved his experimentation; just as certainly she considered *Ulysses* a failure.

If *Mrs. Dalloway* is not an imitation of Joyce's novel, neither does it seem a criticism, inspired or otherwise, except insofar as any novel written by an author aware of his contemporaries and not completely satisfied with their achievements is, by its very difference, a criticism; and in this sense *Mrs. Dalloway* cannot be called a criticism of any other novel in particular.

Both *Ulysses* and *Mrs. Dalloway* take place on one day. Virginia Woolf knew Greek and read the Greek tragedians in the original; *Œdipus Rex* also takes place on one day. In other words, this fact in itself is superficial: what is important is *why* these novels take place on one day, and Joyce's reasons for the unity of time seem very different from Virginia Woolf's. If Joyce used the single day as a unity, Virginia Woolf used it as a diversity. Joyce attempted to show all that a single day can hold; Virginia Woolf, to show that there is no such thing as a single day. Joyce exhausted a day; Virginia Woolf destroyed a day. This is not to say that one was right and one wrong, but only that each was doing a different thing and so employing unity of time for a different reason.

Although *Mrs. Dalloway* does take place on a single day, it does not employ the stream-of-consciousness technique. Virginia Woolf "is generally mentioned as the most refined and lucid exponent of the stream of consciousness method";[48] actually, she never did use it—here or elsewhere—mainly because it was completely out of accord with her "vision."

A stream-of-consciousness passage is a transcription of verbal thought so direct that it seems to bare a human mind. The reader has the illusion of receiving everything; the author creates the illusion of having selected nothing, rejected nothing, corrected nothing. All is given directly from the point of view of the character involved. The famous concluding section of *Ulysses* is a perfect example: it is a singularly interesting record of a singularly uninteresting mind. Joyce's only comment is that there can be no comment; never before was a writer so completely impersonal, and so very much in the way by reason of his utter absence. In *Pilgrimage* Dorothy M. Richardson resorts to dots, either for the sake of clarity; or—what seems more probable—because she conceives the consciousness as blinking, so to speak; or because she is allowing for nonverbal awareness. But Molly Bloom never blinks, and neither does Joyce.

Virginia Woolf, on the other hand, is always present in her novels. The style of her novels coincides perfectly with the vision of life that she saw and that the novels communicate. Beneath the diverse points of view presented to the reader, there is the impersonal narrator—the central intelligence—of which, in and after *Mrs. Dalloway,* the reader is never allowed to become immediately aware, but which extends the idea of a common impulse beneath diversity. The narrator speaks directly, but never in the first person; so that although the reader has often a momentary illusion of entering a character's consciousness, he never "actually does so"—he does not share the characters' thoughts or watch them, but is only told about them. Everything comes second hand. At times, to be sure, the central intelligence is almost completely submerged in the character whose thoughts are being described; then it may rise a little, as the third person singular impersonal pronoun "one" is substituted for the "he" or "she" of the thinker. Daiches says: "Whenever the character is embarked upon a speculation directly relevant to the main theme of the book ... the pronoun tends to be indefinite. ... Thus this very minor device helps Virginia Woolf to make her novels presentations of her own view of life."⁴ The narrator describes a scene or situation, but then he sometimes identifies the description with the impressions of a character. The reader moves with confidence from one character to another, always conscious of the single point of view beneath, but never offensively so, since it is completely impersonal; thus he strings his impressions upon the very thread that is essential for their comprehensive significance. Several of the passages from *Mrs. Dalloway* already quoted will serve to illustrate the method; more subtle examples occurring in the later novels will be given below.

Virginia Woolf proceeded from direct acquaintance to analysis; her reader must proceed from analysis to direct acquaintance. Analysis obviously involves selection; as the narrator says in *Jacob's Room,* "Not exactly what is said, nor yet entirely what is done." In "Phases of Fiction" this idea is expressed somewhat differently. "The enormous growth of the psychological novel in our time has been prompted largely by the mistaken belief . . . that truth is always good; even when it is the truth of the psychoanalyst and not the truth of imagination."[45] The passage goes on to say that although the novel must present "the growth and development of feelings" by copying "the order of the day," it is essential to distinguish between real life and life in the novel—between life and art. Of course all artists select; of course Molly Bloom's stream of consciousness is the result of careful selection, just as Zola's novels are. For Virginia Woolf, the question evidently raised itself as to whether such a passage as the Molly Bloom stream of consciousness is good art, whether the illusion of seeing the "atoms as they fall" is worth the price of so much irrelevance—however important that very irrelevance may be for Joyce's vision.

Virginia Woolf did not, in *Mrs. Dalloway* or elsewhere, use the stream-of-consciousness technique in any exact sense of the term; and it is improbable that Joyce had a direct effect upon either *Mrs. Dalloway* or any other of Virginia Woolf's novels. The two authors saw life from entirely different points of view, despite the fact that both worked in part with Bergsonistic concepts.

Mrs. Dalloway itself, according to one of its critics, is told with "a technical mastery unparalleled in English fiction."[46] If this praise seems excessive, even in the light of Virginia Woolf's own later work, it is true that in *Mrs. Dalloway* Virginia Woolf was able to regulate her perspective and adequately to formalize a consistent interpretation of experience. She herself was not completely satisfied with this novel: her diary shows that she did not especially like Clarissa Dalloway. Even before the novel was published, she was thinking of a new one that she felt to be more subtle, more human, more interesting."[47]

This reaction—this absorption in "some new book which not only thrusts its predecessor from the nest but has a way of subtly blackening its character in comparison with its own"[48]—is the artist's, but not at all necessarily the critic's. It did lead to what can be called Virginia Woolf's creative modulation of the perspective she had now mastered, for *To the Lighthouse* is at once an end in itself and an important step toward something as different from *Mrs. Dalloway* as *Mrs. Dalloway* is different from *The Voyage Out*.

CHAPTER IV

THE CREATIVE MODULATION OF PERSPECTIVE

TRUE LIFE exists where the living being is conscious of itself as an indivisible "I," in whom all impressions, feelings, etc., become one. So long as the "I" struggles, as nearly the whole animal world does, merely to crush the other creatures known to him, in order to attain his own temporary advantage, true spiritual life which is without time and space remains unexpressed and imprisoned. True spiritual life is liberated when a man neither rejoices in his own happiness, nor suffers from his own suffering, but suffers and rejoices with the worries and pleasures of others and is fused with them into a common life....

There are two consciousnesses in us: one—the animal; the other—the spiritual. The spiritual is not always shown in us, but it is this that makes our true spiritual life, which is not subject to time.... there are times in my long life which are clearly preserved in my memory, and other times which have completely disappeared, they no longer exist. The moments which remain are most frequently the moments when the spirit in me awoke.... Spiritual life is a recollection. A recollection is not the past, it is always the present. It is our spirit, which shows itself more or less clearly, that contains the progress of man's temporary existence. There can be no progress for the spirit, for it is not in time. What the life in time is for, we do not know; it is only a transitory phenomenon. Speaking metaphorically, I see this manifestation of the spirit in us as the breathing of God.[1]

Even if it were not known that Virginia Woolf herself translated these remarks of Tolstoi, their affinity to *Mrs. Dalloway* would be obvious. But there is a shift in emphasis between the first and second paragraphs of this passage—a shift from spiritual life to spirit itself, from definition to illustration. A shift similar to this constitutes the first step in what can be understood as Virginia Woolf's creative modulation of her perspective. Having given artistic definition to her vision of experience, having realized a total *donnée,* Virginia Woolf was now able to manipulate that formal perspective in various ways; and thus she was modulating the philosophical perspective as well, discovering new angles, new emphases, new modes, with each new construct. *Mrs. Dalloway* defines—but *To the Lighthouse* illustrates—her own concept of reality.

To the Lighthouse was published in 1927, twelve years after *The Voyage Out.* It is divided into three main parts: "The Window," "Time Passes," and "The Lighthouse." The first part is concerned with the events of one evening and night in mid-September of about 1910, and the third part with the events of one morning ten years later. Unity of place is preserved throughout, and the setting is at once precise and vague. It is a house at Finlay in the Skye Islands; but when Paul Rayley thinks of slipping out of the house early in the morning to go all the way to Edinburgh and replace a brooch that Minta Doyle has lost, the reader may begin to think—although Paul's state of mind might account for his resolve—of the notorious seacoast of Bohemia in *The Winter's Tale;* however, Virgina Woolf too was notorious for her lack of attention to factual accuracy,[2] and the exact scene of the action is unimportant.

Indeed, the action itself might be considered equally unimportant. In the first part of the book James Ramsay wishes to go to the lighthouse, but cannot because of bad weather; in the third part he finally makes the journey, but against his will. This is the central action of the novel. Parallel to it runs the progress of Lily Briscoe's painting. At first she cannot formalize her vision upon canvas; finally she succeeds in completing the picture, but not at all to her satisfaction. The climax of the novel—Mrs. Ramsay's death—is mentioned very casually in a parenthetical sentence; the catastrophe—Mr. Ramsay's arrival at the lighthouse and Lily's completion of her painting—comes as an exhausted afterthought. No act, no event can be pinned down: even Mrs. Ramsay's dinner party, by far the longest scene in the book, is not self-contained, for it concludes with her own realization that the party had begun to end some time ago. Not an act or a series of acts, but action itself—movement rather than movements—is described by this novel.

The characters themselves are for the most part seen in action: Mr. Ramsay pacing up and down the terrace, Cam running wildly and stopping only at her mother's call. In this movement three things alone remain fixed: Mrs. Ramsay, the lighthouse, and Lily's painting. Even these must not be labeled, for "nothing was simply one thing." So, for example, even the lighthouse is both stark and misty. Arriving at the lighthouse, James remembers it as he had seen it when he was a child of six:

The Lighthouse was then a silvery, misty-looking tower with a yellow eye, that opened suddenly, and softly in the evening. Now—

James looked at the Lighthouse. He could see the white-washed rocks; the tower, stark and straight; he could see that it was barred with black and white; he could see windows in it; he could even see washing spread on the rocks to dry. So that was the Lighthouse, was it?

No, the other was also the Lighthouse. For nothing was simply one thing. The other Lighthouse was true too.

This very important passage serves to comment upon the numerous interpretations of the lighthouse symbol. Almost every critic explains the lighthouse differently—and almost every critic makes what would seem to be the mistake of finding the lighthouse "simply one thing." H. K. Russell declares that the lighthouse is the feminine creative principle; that Mrs. Ramsay equals Bergson's "intuition" equals Joyce's "Anna Livia Plurabelle."[3] Joan Bennett calls the alternate light and shadow of the lighthouse the rhythm of joy and sorrow, understanding and misunderstanding.[4] Daiches says: "The Lighthouse ... standing lonely in the midst of the sea, is a symbol of the individual who is at once a unique being and a part of the flux of history. To reach the Lighthouse is, in a sense, to make contact with a truth outside oneself, to surrender the uniqueness of one's ego to an impersonal reality"[5]—surely a worth-while comment. F. L.

Overcarsh, in a detailed interpretation of the novel, avoids calling the lighthouse simply one thing. He finds the novel as a whole an allegory of the Old and New Testaments; Mrs. Ramsay is Eve, the Blessed Virgin, and Christ; Mr. Ramsay is, among other things, God the Father; the lighthouse is Eden and Heaven; the strokes of the lighthouse are the Persons of the Trinity, the third of them, long and steady, representing the Holy Ghost.[6] Perhaps more precise than any of these interpretations is John Graham's statement that the lighthouse as symbol has no one meaning, that it is "a vital synthesis of time and eternity: an objective correlative for Mrs. Ramsay's vision, after whose death it is her meaning."[7]

Mrs. Ramsay is of course the central character, and one of Virginia Woolf's most successful creations. She is projected more as a symbol than as an individual: she is never called by a first name, for example, and she wears gray clothes during the day and black at night, so that the reader is given the odd impression of looking at once upon and through her whenever she appears. Despite this intentional indefiniteness, Mrs. Ramsay emerges as a human being of great appeal, though the facts about her are symbolical as well as literal. She is an extremely beautiful woman of fifty, an inveterate matchmaker, and the mother of eight children; she is very nearsighted; she exaggerates everything; she is a practical nurse, and much concerned with the improvement of social conditions. Like Clarissa Dalloway (and Terence Hewet), Mrs. Ramsay can create moments of unity that remain intact in the memory, "affecting one almost like a work of art."

Mr. Ramsay, her husband, has been generally looked upon as something of a villain. He is eleven years older than his wife, and a teacher of philosophy possessed of a superb intellect. He is long-sighted, precisely factual, and pessimistic. Certainly he is Mrs. Ramsay's opposite, but he "is not a figure of fun,"[8] as many critics have thought him. He is, to be sure, suggestive of Leslie

Stephen, notably in his habit of shouting out poetry to himself and his detestation of the long dinner parties at which his wife is so good a hostess. Q. D. Leavis says: "Everyone has read *To the Lighthouse,* and the portrait-piece of Mr. Ramsay by Leslie Stephen's gifted daughter elicited immediate recognition from the oldest generation. Yes, that's Leslie Stephen, the word went round; and that brilliant study in the Lytton Strachey manner of a slightly ludicrous, slightly bogus, Victorian philosopher somehow served to discredit Leslie Stephen's literary work. But it is obvious to any student of it that the work could not have been produced by Mr. Ramsay."[9] Then it should also be obvious that Virginia Woolf had no intention of ridiculing her father or Mr. Ramsay, whose eccentricities are no more meant to be belittling than are those of his wife. Mr. Ramsay is admirable, if not always correct; he is human, but not evil.[10]

The essential difference between Mr. and Mrs. Ramsay is that whereas he identifies himself with the land and thinks the sea a destroyer, she—like Lily Briscoe—believes that life is the sea and not the land. Thus Mrs. Ramsay "felt ... that community of feeling with other people which emotion gives as if the walls of partition had become so still that practically (the feeling was one of relief and happiness) it was all one stream, and chairs, tables, maps, were hers, were theirs, it did not matter whose, and [they] would carry it on when she was dead." Lily, the artist, sees "how life, from being made up of little separate incidents which one lives one by one, became curled and whole like a wave which bore one up with it and threw one down with it, there, with a dash on the beach." Mr. Ramsay thinks of "the dark of human ignorance, how we know nothing and the sea eats away the ground we stand on." For him, and for James, "loneliness ... was ... the truth about things." In the same way, Mr. Ramsay is afraid that he will be forgot, that time will destroy his work; Mrs. Ramsay, however, since she does not draw a line around her individuality, does not fear time; and Lily finishes her painting, even though she knows that it will never be displayed, because "one might say, even of this scrawl, not of that actual picture, perhaps, but of what it attempted, that it 'remained for ever.'"

To the Lighthouse is really the story of a contest between two kinds of truth—Mr. Ramsay's and Mrs. Ramsay's. For him, truth is factual truth; for her, truth is the movement toward truth: since truth is always *being* made, and never *is* made, the struggle for truth is the truth itself. The form of this novel at once expresses and verifies Mrs. Ramsay's truth. According to Bergson, certainty can follow only from factual extension of knowledge resulting in scientific order; such is the order which Mr. Ramsay seeks. Mr. Ramsay spatializes knowledge:

If thought is like the keyboard of a piano, divided into as many notes, or like the alphabet is ranged in twenty-six letters all in order, then his splendid mind had no sort of difficulty in running over those letters one by one, firmly and accurately, until it had reached, say, the letter Q. He reached Q.... But after Q? What comes next? After Q there are a number of letters the last of which is scarcely visible to mortal eyes, but glimmers red in the distance. Z is only reached once by one man in a generation. Still, if he could reach R it would be something.

Here is a logical, scientific procedure toward truth.

Mrs. Ramsay, on the other hand, knows by intuition rather than by analysis, and is therefore able to know reality—mobility, qualitative rather than quantitative diversity, time instead of space, movement itself and not merely the path of movement in space.

Matter ... has no duration and so cannot last through any period of time or change: it simply *is* in the present, it does not endure but is perpetually destroyed and recreated.... Just as matter is absolute logical complexity memory is absolute creative synthesis. Together they constitute the hybrid notion of creative duration whose "parts" interpenetrate which, according to Bergson, comes nearest to giving a satisfactory description of the actual fact directly known which is, for him, the whole reality.[11]

Mr. Ramsay—matter—and Lily Briscoe—memory—undergo such an "interpenetration" in the novel's catastrophe, and by doing so give a satisfactory description of Mrs. Ramsay's truth.

"The Window" is a statement of that truth. This first part of the novel seems complete in itself. It begins: " 'Yes, of course, if it's fine tomorrow,' said Mrs. Ramsay"; and concludes, again with Mrs. Ramsay speaking: " 'Yes, you were right. It's going to be wet tomorrow. You won't be able to go.' " The conflict is projected as a question about the weather. It is a fact, stated by Mr. Ramsay at once, that " 'it won't be fine.' " Charles Tansley—"the little atheist," as he is called—backs up this fact. But Mrs. Ramsay will not accept it as truth, because it hurts James, who wants nothing more than to go out to the lighthouse. Instead she says, " 'But it may be fine—I expect it will be fine,' " and calls her husband's fact nonsense. At the conclusion of this part, when she agrees with her husband that it will rain tomorrow, it is not because she attaches importance to his truth, but because she knows that he wishes her to say "I love you," and chooses to say it in this way. In neither case is the fact itself of any importance whatsoever to her.

Her disregard of factual truth enrages Mr. Ramsay. After all, he *is* right. Mrs. Ramsay's truth is one that must trample upon her husband's, however; but his truth—factual truth—is so short-lived that she can distort or deny it without compunction. He himself realizes its fragility; in a generation, he thinks, he will be forgot; even Shakespeare will some day be forgot. It is for this reason that his wife is so essential to him; although he "exaggerated her ignorance, her simplicity, for he liked to think that she was not clever, not book-learned at all," he nevertheless "wanted, to be assured of his genius, first of all, and then to be taken within the circle of life, warmed and soothed, to have his senses restored to him, his barrenness made fertile, and all the rooms of the house be made full of life.... He must be assured that he too lived in the heart of life." Therefore he must from time to time leave off his metaphysical speculations and return to his wife, to "life itself," for sympathy; Mrs. Ramsay can communicate to her husband that "if he put his implicit faith in her, nothing should hurt him; however deep he buried himself or climbed high, not for a second should he find himself without her. So boasting of her capacity to surround and protect, there was scarcely a shell of herself left for her to know herself by; all was so lavished and spent." Mrs. Ramsay's apparent illogicality is actually the certainty of intuition. For her husband her truth is a false truth, but without it he would perish. "She knew then—she knew without having learnt. Her simplicity fathomed what clever people falsified. Her singleness of mind made her drop plumb like a stone, alight exact as a bird, gave her, naturally, this swoop and fall of the spirit upon truth which delighted, eased, sustained—falsely perhaps." "Falsely perhaps," because her perception of true time has not yet been proved correct. She has been seen only through a window, and the reader has seen her concept of truth only through the window of her own "room." She has identified her truth with the lighthouse. "There is a coherence in things, a stability; something . . . is immune from change, and shines out . . . in the face of the flowing, the fleeting, the spectral, like a ruby"; this can be glimpsed at certain moments, and "of such moments, she thought, the thing is made that endures." Just as Mr. Ramsay's Z "glimmers red in the distance," so the "something" that Mrs. Ramsay feels stable shines like a ruby. Her way of meeting it is different from her husband's way—hers being really an end, and his a means. "Losing personality, one lost the fret, the hurry, the stir . . . things came together in this peace, this rest, this eternity; and pausing there she looked out to meet that stroke of the Lighthouse, the long steady stroke, the last of the three, which was her stroke."

Seven times in this part of the novel, the phrase "Someone had blundered" is repeated. Either Mr. Ramsay or Mrs. Ramsay is wrong, and the remainder of the novel shows that it is Mr. Ramsay who "had blundered."

The short second part, "Time Passes," has been praised by almost every critic of the novel as a masterpiece of description. According to Brewster and Burrell, "It would be hard to find anything in twentieth century English prose to surpass [this part]";[12] others join them in ranking it one of the great passages of English prose. This is all very well, but to remove the part from the whole is to run the risk of ignoring its function. "Time Passes" must not be thought of as a piece of impressionistic writing; it is actually the testing of Mrs. Ramsay's vision by Mr. Ramsay's facts, and the apparent triumph of those facts. Simply, it describes the effects of ten years' time upon the little house. The books become moldy; Mrs. Ramsay's beloved garden is choked with weeds; toads, swallows, and mice invade the rooms; the wood rots; above all, Mrs. Ramsay's truth—symbolized by the shawl she had wrapped around a frightening skull in the children's bedroom—falls victim to "the facts." Gradually the folds of the shawl loosen, so that the skull emerges a skull, and not the fairy garden she had called it when it annoyed Cam and James. There is no eternity, no permanence; there are only dust, death, decay. Indeed, Mrs. Ramsay herself dies during this ten-year interval; her son Andrew is killed in the war; her daughter Prue dies in childbirth (just as Mrs. Ramsay had lived for childbirth). It would seem, then, that Mr. Ramsay was correct, for the facts of this spatialized time confirm his pessimism and prove his wife's optimism illusory. When Mrs. McNab, who has come now and then to dust the empty house, is suddenly asked to have it ready for occupancy, she labors for days with two other workers to repair the ravages of time. Finally Mr. Ramsay, the remaining children, Lily, and Mr. Carmichael (who has become a famous poet despite his addiction to drugs) return.

"Le temps passe, et peu à peu tout ce qu'on disait par

mensonge devient vrai,"[13] wrote Proust. "The Lighthouse" is, in a sense, testimony to this statement, for here Mrs. Ramsay's "lies" are proved to have been—and still to be—the truth, capable of refuting Mr. Ramsay's "facts." Time passes, and yet true time does not pass.

Throughout the first part of the novel, Lily Briscoe had been absorbed in her attempt to capture reality in a painting. She did not see the scene as the fashionable Mr. Paunceforte had painted it. He had rendered the violent colors about her as pastels, and it was now the custom to see them as he had seen them, to ignore the reality. Despite Paunceforte's distortion, Lily managed "to clasp some miserable remnant of her vision to her breast, which a thousand forces did their best to pluck from her."[14] In Lily's picture the real and not the apparent Mrs. Ramsay was to be captured; Mrs. Ramsay there was represented abstractly as a triangular purple shape (the shadow that, seated in the window, she cast upon the step), and not as a woman in a gray dress. Indeed, Mrs. Ramsay thought of herself as "a wedge-shaped core of darkness, something invisible to others"; and it was this wedge-shaped core, she felt, that would remain permanent and eternal.

Lily had been unable to complete her painting. "A mother and child might be reduced to a shadow without irreverence. A light here required a shadow there." But she could not solve the problem of form: "Mrs. Ramsay ... as she sat in the wicker arm-chair in the drawing-room window ... wore, to Lily's eyes, an august shape; the shape of a dome.... It was a question, [Lily] remembered, how to connect this mass on the right hand with that on the left."

Now, ten years later, Lily tries again to capture her vision by formalizing it. Her attitude at the beginning of the third part enables the reader to become aware of the symbolic meanings of the circumstance. "The question was of some relation between those masses," and Lily now feels that she has the solution. The painting causes her to remember Mrs. Ramsay, and to recall certain moments of the past. Meanwhile Mr. Ramsay comes to her demanding the sympathy his wife used to give him, but Lily can do nothing except remark that his boots are beautiful—just as Mrs. Flanders had evaded the central problem in *Jacob's Room* by switching her attention to Jacob's shoes.

Mr. Ramsay leaves for the lighthouse, and Lily begins her painting. "Here she was again, she thought, stepping back to look at it, drawn out of gossip, out of living, out of community with people into the presence of this formidable ancient enemy of hers—this other thing, this truth, this reality, which suddenly...emerged stark at the back of appearances and commanded her attention." More and more she thinks of Mrs. Ramsay as she continues to paint.

Pour entrer en nous, un être a été obligé de prendre la forme, de se plier au cadre du temps; ne nous apparaissant que par minutes successives, il n'a jamais pu nous livrer de lui qu'un seul aspect à la fois, nous débiter de lui qu'une seule photographie. Grande faiblesse sans doute pour un être de consister en une simple collection de moments; grande force aussi; il relève de la mémoire, et la mémoire d'un moment n'est pas instruite de tout ce qui s'est passé depuis; ce moment qu'elle a enregistré dure encore, vit encore et avec lui l'être qui s'y profilait. Et puis cet émiettement ne fait pas seulement vivre la morte, il la multiplie.[15]

In just the same way, Mrs. Ramsay rises from death and lives again. Lily, as she paints, "exchanged the fluidity of life for the concentration of painting"; she loses consciousness of her personality, her name, her separateness. She remembers Mrs. Ramsay

bringing them together; Mrs. Ramsay saying, "Life stand still here"; Mrs. Ramsay making of the moment something permanent (as in another sphere Lily herself tried to make of the moment something permanent)—this was of the nature of a revelation. In the midst of chaos there was shape; this eternal passing and flowing (she looked at the clouds going and the leaves shaking) was struck into stability. Life stand still here, Mrs. Ramsey said....She owed it all to her.

What Mrs. Ramsay had accomplished with the living moment, like a misty or a stark tower holding the light still and illumining with it, Lily is accomplishing with her painting. Lily cries out for Mrs. Ramsay to come back, to return; but "nothing happened," for "the vision must be perpetually remade." She wants to get hold of "the thing itself before it has been made anything" and so to give it expression from its source. She goes on thinking of Mrs. Ramsay, bringing the past into the present in a recollection in tranquillity.

Suddenly the window at which she was looking was whitened by some light stuff behind it. At last then somebody had come into the drawing-room; somebody was sitting in the chair.... Mercifully, whoever it was ... had settled by some stroke of luck so as to throw an odd-shaped triangular shadow over the step.... One must keep on looking without for a second relaxing the intensity of emotion, the determination not to be put off, not to be bamboozled. One must hold the scene—so—in a vise and let nothing come in and spoil it.

Lily too is saying, "Life stand still here." Then, quietly, it is Mrs. Ramsay sitting at the window. Lily finishes her painting. "Yes, she thought, laying down her brush in extreme fatigue, I have had my vision." Lily has made her journey to the lighthouse.

Mr. Ramsay's own journey to the lighthouse, accompanied by James and Cam, is naturally a literal and factual one. He reads a book during the voyage, and finishes reading it as the boat arrives at the literal lighthouse. He has, so to speak, reached Z by making this trip in memory of his wife—by forcing James finally to go to the lighthouse. During this third part of the novel, the phrase "We perished, each alone" is repeated just as "Some one had blundered" was repeated in the first part. Mr. Ramsay reaches the lighthouse. "He sat and looked at the island and he might be thinking, We perished, each alone, or he might be thinking, I have reached it. I have found it; but he said nothing. Then he put on his hat.... he sprang, lightly like a young man, holding his parcel, on to the rock." During the journey to the lighthouse, Mr. Ramsay has been hearing of the terrible shipwrecks caused by a storm in the winter. He himself, however, carrying a package of presents for the lighthouse man, has finally been able to communicate, to give instead of take, to reach the lighthouse.

The novel itself is comparable to Lily's painting, for its purpose too is to capture and render stable and permanent the essence of Mrs. Ramsay. For a long time Lily "could not achieve that razor edge of balance between two opposite forces; Mr. Ramsay and the picture; which was necessary. There was something perhaps wrong with the design? Was it ... that the line of the wall wanted breaking?" The third part of the novel does precisely what Lily's finished painting does: it connects the masses—matter and memory—and by connecting them is able to illustrate "life itself" as Virginia Woolf envisioned it. Moving from Lily to Mr. Ramsay and back, "The Lighthouse" not only explains but also dynamically depicts the process by which "life itself" is discovered.

There is an interesting and perhaps not entirely superficial resemblance between *To the Lighthouse* and E. M. Forster's *Howards End*. As in *To the Lighthouse*, the house Howards End is a unifying force in Forster's novel. It is occupied during Ruth Wilcox's life, then empty and cared for by Miss Avery, then occupied again. Further, Ruth Wilcox dominates *Howards End*, although she dies early in the book. Forster's dualism of love and truth—the passion and the prose—although not identical with the matter-memory of *To the Lighthouse*, is nevertheless the cause of a similar pattern. Forster's *Where Angels Fear to Tread* also carries a hint—not nearly so important as Proust's—of the problem treated here. If Forster offers a suggestion, the way in which Marcel's mother "becomes" his dead grandmother in *Sodome et Gomorrhe*—mentally re-creating and rediscovering her—is of course a far more significant suggestion of Lily's re-creation of Mrs. Ramsay.

The role of the narrator or central intelligence is both more important and less noticeable in *To the Lighthouse* than in *Mrs. Dalloway*. As in the earlier novel, the narrator is a means by which the reader attains a unity of response to the diverse personalities within whose consciousnesses he has the illusion of being; he is objectively unconscious of a narrator, but the narrator makes possible both the artistic validity of the novel's statement and his acceptance of it. Far from being a stream-of-consciousness novel, *To the Lighthouse* is the objective account of a central intelligence that approaches and assumes the characters' consciousnesses (just as Clarissa and Mrs. Ramsay enjoin themselves vicariously to all life) but does not become completely identified with any one consciousness. This central intelligence is thus free to comment upon the whole in what seems a completely impersonal manner, as this short passage shows:

"It is a triumph," said Mr. Bankes, laying his knife down for a moment. He had eaten attentively. It was rich; it was tender. It was perfectly cooked. How did she manage these things in the depths of the country? he asked her. She was a wonderful woman. All his love, all his reverence, had returned; and she knew it.

"It is a French recipe of my grandmother's," said Mrs. Ramsey, speaking with a ring of great pleasure in her voice. Of course it was French. What passes for cookery in England is an abomination (they agreed). It is putting cabbages in water. It is roasting meat until it is like leather. It is cutting off the delicious skins of vegetables. "In which," said Mr. Bankes, "all the virtue of the vegetable is contained."

Here the central intelligence is reporting a part of the dinner conversation. The remark in parentheses is a popular device by which the author assures the reader that she too agrees with what is being said. The sentences that follow are both a digest of the conversation and an opinion expressed by the central intelligence; the reader, regarding them as an oblique report of the conversation, also reacts toward what the people say with a sympathy seemingly caused by the situation—he has been hoping that Mr. Bankes will approve the *bœuf en daube*—but actually caused by the informing personality of the central intelligence. Further, "She was a wonderful woman" is read as Bankes' thought; "All his love ..." is somewhere between his thought and a statement by the narrator, being in the third person; "and she knew it" is, finally, a direct transitional statement by the central intelligence. But the illusion is so well sustained that Mr. Bankes' final remark (" 'In which ... all the virtue ...' ") seems to spring only from an abstract of the conversation. Thus the technique serves to instill a common reaction into the diverse reactions of the characters—to affect precisely that unity in diversity of the theme—and so to make certain the reader's response to the book as a whole. It is also compatible with Virginia Woolf's idea of characterization: her belief that there is a common element beneath the diversity, that fundamentally it is "all one stream." For this reason Virginia Woolf "learnt to ... annihilate the clear line between narrator and character, creating mind and created scene, to take the frame from the picture. ... to make of all—time, place, person, self and other self—a unity. ..."[16]

Most critics consider *To the Lighthouse* Virginia Woolf's masterpiece, mainly because of the technical ability it displays, the unity of effect, masterful structure. Often it is described in the words with which Lily Briscoe thinks of her painting: "Beautiful and bright it should be on the surface, feathery and evanescent, one colour melting into another like the colours on a butterfly's wing; but beneath the fabric must be clamped together with bolts of iron. It was to be a thing you could ruffle with your breath; and a thing you could not dislodge with a team of horses." This novel also fulfills, in the use to which it puts its materials, Lily's postimpressionistic intention that "one wanted ... to be on a level with ordinary experience, to feel simply that's a chair, that's a table, and yet at the same time, It's a miracle, it's an ecstasy." As she was finishing this novel, Virginia Woolf considered it by far her best—more subtle and human than *Jacob's Room* or *Mrs. Dalloway*, more interesting, more successful in method. But she was already thinking of a further development of that method, and had a vague idea for a book in which time would be completely abolished, "my theory being that the actual event practically does not exist—nor time either."[17] This theory she also developed, and only one year after *To the Lighthouse* she published, in 1928, her next novel, *Orlando, a Biography*.

Orlando is a fantasy that moves in time from about 1586 to October 11, 1928; its action takes place in England and the Near East. The hero-heroine Orlando grows, during 342 years, from an Elizabethan boy of sixteen to a twentieth-century woman of thirty-six. As a boy, Orlando catches the fancy of Queen Elizabeth I and is made her treasurer and steward; but he is exiled from court for failing to marry the Lady Margaret O'Brien O'Dare O'Reilley Tyrconnel (alias Euphrosyne), who had compared unfavorably with the beautiful but faithless Princess Marousha Stanislovska Dagmar Natasha Iliana Romanovitch (alias Sasha). To escape the lust of Archduchess Harriet Griselda of Finster-Aarhorn and Scandop-Boom in the Romanian territory, Orlando becomes Ambassador to Turkey, where he negotiates between Charles II and the Turks; as a reward for his invaluable services, he is given a dukedom. Awaking one morning after a trance of over a week, Orlando finds himself become a woman. Obviously unable to continue as ambassador, she joins a gypsy tribe; but since her love of nature is considered most unconventional in that community, she returns to England aboard the *Enamoured Lady,* an English merchant ship, and settles down at her huge ancestral estate. Orlando's return sets in motion a series of law suits that, in true English fashion, take more than a hundred years to settle, and as results of which she is pronounced indisputably a woman and her three sons by the

Spanish dancer Rosina Pepita are declared illegitimate. The Archduchess Harriet—who now reveals himself as really the Archduke Harry—continues to annoy Orlando; by cheating at Fly Loo and dropping a toad inside his shirt, Orlando manages to rid herself of him, and goes to London—to Blackfriars—for the purpose of finding life and a lover. There she has a series of adventures that include joining the fashionable salons, meeting Pope and Addison, falling in love for a time with another woman, and changing her sex (clothes) often in order to heighten her enjoyment of life and to widen her experience. With the advent of the Victorian period, however, Orlando hurriedly changes from eighteenth- to nineteenth-century clothes and becomes "a real woman at last." She marries Marmaduke Bonthrop Shelmerdine, Esquire, who leaves immediately after the ceremony to continue his career of sailing around Cape Horn. Orlando gives birth to her first child (a boy) and wins the Burdett Coutts Memorial Prize for her poem "The Oak Tree," which she had begun in 1586. Otherwise—aside from the fact that her house has 365 bedrooms—Orlando is just like any other twentieth-century woman.

Of course *Orlando* has been given innumerable interpretations. It has been called "a study in multiple personality, and a protest against the too narrow labeling of anybody";[18] "a dynamic fantasia on the history of England's spirit";[19] "une histoire raccourcie de la littérature anglaise";[20] "a learned parable of literary criticism";[21] "a fantastic meditation on a portrait of Victoria Sackville-West."[22] Ruth Gruber, calling it a satire on criticism, adds that it "seems as much the history of [Virginia Woolf's] own literary growth as that of Miss Sackville-West or of England. Virginia Woolf appears to trace her poetic development from that of a romantic child to a woman seeking the realities modulated by her sex."[23] All these statements about *Orlando* can be called true. None of them, however, is true for the book as a whole: none of them can be—or should be—used in the attempt to "interpret" each scene or sentence on a single level. It is true, for example, that Orlando's clothes usually correspond to the poetic style of each period, so that at the beginning of the Victorian period she realizes that a person can no longer "still say what one liked and wear knee-breeches or skirts as the fancy took one," and so hurries home to escape embarrassment and "wrapped herself as well as she could in a damask quilt which she snatched from her bed" until she can procure suitable clothes. But it would be a subjective view indeed that attempted to "interpret" Orlando's son upon the same level. If "nothing was simply one thing" in *To the Lighthouse,* the same is true in *Orlando.* Orlando herself thinks that "nothing is any longer one thing," that "everything was partly something else." These are thoughts of the twentieth-century Orlando. In the past a thing was simply one thing, so that the "old" Orlando was a relatively simple person; the "new," the modern Orlando, however, is composed of many selves that form a complex whole. It is in terms of this Orlando—of the time at which Virginia Woolf wrote the book—that meaning must be understood. Therefore it follows that *Orlando* cannot be explained as an imaginative biography of Victoria Sackville-West or of English poetry or of the English spirit, but that these partial meanings are ways to the book's total meaning rather than ends in themselves. If *Orlando* were a consistent parable or allegory upon any one of these levels, if it were explicable according to some one fixed symbol, it would be false to the whole concept that determined it.

  Orlando is a fantasy and an allegory only on the surface; as an expression of its thought, the technique is functional and not mere virtuoso caprice. *Orlando* is just as serious as *To the Lighthouse,* but, by further creative modulation of her perspective, Virginia Woolf was able to accomplish her serious meaning through a humorous form, and so to comment upon it in a new way—to explore new possibilities of its implications.

Like *Jacob's Room, Orlando* has two narrators; but here the device is used purely for its ironic value; there is never any doubt that the prim and coy man who is writing Orlando's biography is himself a comment upon himself—a comment made by the central intelligence who, through most of the novel, backs away from the biographer so that he becomes part of the total perspective. Throughout, this biographer insists that he is writing a biography and not a novel. As soon as Orlando begins to think, the biographer begins to apologize: "These are not matters upon which a biographer can profitably enlarge"; "life, the... authorities have decided, has nothing whatever to do with... thinking. Thought and life are as the poles asunder." Just as he is ashamed of thought and imagination, he is very proud when he can describe action or muster facts; thus he is careful to quote from diaries and letters, and to give his readers most detail about what is least important: he does not mention even the year of Orlando's birth, but he is careful to note that Nick Greene visited Orlando "punctually at seven o'clock on Monday, April the twenty-first," or that it was June 16th, 1712, when Orlando said, " 'What the devil is the matter with me?' " He is often ashamed of Orlando's exploits; "Let other pens," he alludes to Jane Austen, "speak of sex and sexuality; we quit such odious subjects as soon as we can." This biographer is responsible for the pedantic footnotes; parts of the fussy, scholarly preface, with its ridiculous statements; the hopelessly incomplete index, with such entries as "Abbey, Westminster," "Frost, the Great," and "Keynes, Mrs. J. M. (*see* Lopokova, Madame)." Of these, the preface is perhaps most successful, combining as it does factual and ironic truth; of the sixty-odd persons whom the author thanks here, some merit thanks and others anything but thanks.

This device of the author's is the first example of Virginia Woolf's extended use of comic irony. Irony is in all the novels, but it has usually serious overtones and only at times a suggestion of humor; here the comic value of the irony makes it seem to be all the more truthful and effective in its criticism. Clearly, that criticism is not only of clock time but of knowledge dependent upon clock time. The biographer is, as Mr. Ramsay was not, ludicrous in his valiant attempts to arrive at truth by using facts—and facts only. Just as "when the shrivelled skin of the ordinary is stuffed out with meaning it satisfies the senses amazingly," so when fact is played upon by imagination it satisfies the intellect. The chronological order of *Orlando*—the procedure from period to period of English history in perfect logical order—is completely nullified by the last fifteen pages, in which the action proper of the novel may be said to begin and in which the past is recapitulated temporally rather than spatially, so that the past becomes present, the present past, and, as Virginia Woolf had noted in her diary, "the actual event practically does not exist." Driving home along the Old Kent Road, on October 11, 1928, Orlando is at once all that he-she has been during more than three hundred years. Bergson said: "Is my own person, at a given moment, one or manifold? If I declare it one, inner voices arise and protest—those of the sensations, feelings, ideas, among which my individuality is distributed. But, if I make it distinctly manifold, my consciousness rebels quite as strongly; it affirms that my sensations, my feelings, my thoughts are abstractions which I effect on myself, and that each of my states implies all the others." The actual state, the present event, is made actual and present only by being fixed intellectually in space; on the other hand, "intuition is mind itself, and, in a certain sense, life itself: the intellect has been cut out of it by a process resembling that which has generated matter. Thus is revealed the unity of the spiritual life. We recognize it only when we place ourselves in intuition in order to go from intuition to the intellect, for from the intellect we shall never pass to intuition."[24] The first five chapters of *Orlando* are what the intellect perceives; in the last chapter there is the intuitive perception of Orlando in which all

that has been spatially ranged by the intellect is temporally unified by the intuition. Since the intuition does not halt or fix the
actual event, but instead perceives its pure-time duration, the
actual event "practically does not exist." There is no past, no
present, no future, but only pure duration itself, one and undivided. This is the truth, the wild goose that the biographer has
been chasing and that suddenly appears on the last page of the
novel.

Time and personality are fused in this book:

For if there are (at a venture) seventy-six different times all ticking
in the mind at once, how many different people are there not—
Heaven help us—all having lodgment at one time or another in the
human spirit? Some say two thousand and fifty-two. . . . she had a
great variety of selves to call upon, far more than we have been able
to find room for, since a biography is considered complete if it merely
accounts for six or seven selves, whereas a person may well have as
many thousand. Choosing, then, only those selves we have found
room for, Orlando may now have called on the boy who cut the
nigger's head down; the boy who strung it up again; the boy who
sat on the hill; the boy who saw the poet.

But Orlando wants the "true self," "as happens when . . . the
conscious self, which is the uppermost, and has the power to
desire, wishes to be nothing but one self." There follows a
monologue that comes as close to being "stream of consciousness" as anything Virginia Woolf ever wrote, but it is interrupted constantly by comment from the author. It is only when
Orlando stops sorting her selves—she is in despair, as Bernard
will be in *The Waves,* because she can make words and phrases
but never catch the thing itself—when she stops separating and
spatializing the different parts of her personality, that she finds
the Orlando for whom she has been searching. "She was now
darkened, stilled, and become, with the addition of this Orlando,
what is called, rightly or wrongly, a single self, a real self. And
she fell silent. For it is probable that when people talk aloud the
selves (of which there may be more than two thousand) are

conscious of disseverment, and are trying to communicate, but when communication is established they fall silent." The real Orlando, then, is simply the communication of all these different and diverse Orlandos. When that communication has been accomplished, it is "as if her mind had become a fluid that flowed round things and enclosed them completely." Now, when the clock strikes the hour, Orlando can withstand its shock better than she could in London earlier in the day, "for she was now one and entire, and presented, it may be, a larger surface to the shock of time." Gradually the striking of the clock comes to have less and less alarm for her, because she remains "a real self"; and it is in spite of clock time—at the very moment indeed when the strokes of midnight are sounding—that she finally finds the wild goose.

This awareness of Orlando is the reason for all that has gone before it; one by one the selves have been perceived spatially; one self is at last perceived intuitively. In this sense, *Orlando* occupies only the one day in 1928, and from it are projected back into space the three hundred years of its first five chapters; just as all these different times are one time, so all Orlando's different selves are one self. On the other hand, just as the one self is actually a way of seeing innumerable selves—a communication of the selves—so the moment at which Orlando's awareness becomes complete and one is actually a communication of innumerable other moments—again, the actual event does not exist. As in the novels preceding it, in *Orlando* unity is the essence of diversity itself; but in *Orlando* there is, as Delattre has noted, not only duration and memory but also intellect and irony.[25] It is from the ironical presentation of clock time that the novel proceeds to its affirmation of duration and memory; before its theme can be fully revealed, however, that intuitive perception must in turn be intellectualized. This is of course quite in accord with Bergson's statement: "Intuition and intellect represent two opposite directions of the work of consciousness: intuition goes in the very direction of life, intellect goes in the inverse direction, and thus finds itself naturally in accordance with the movement of matter. A complete and perfect humanity would be that in which these two forms of conscious activity should attain their full development."[26]

Although *Orlando* has been compared to *As You Like It* and even to *Orlando Furioso*,[27] very little if anything seems to have been gained by such comparisons. At least one of the many *stylistic* echoes in this novel is probably of more than casual significance. It is well known that appropriate imitations of the great English prose stylists occur throughout the book; yet imitations of Laurence Sterne can be found, not only in chapter iv, which deals with the eighteenth century, but also in every other chapter. The Sternesque touches are used by Virginia Woolf to underline the meaning of the total novel as well as to capture the flavor of the eighteenth century.[28] With some important differences, Sterne and Virginia Woolf were remarkably alike in philosophical perspective; it is not surprising, then, that when she employed comic irony to show the illogicality of logic, Virginia Woolf should avail herself of Sterne's methods. Mr. Ramsay of *To the Lighthouse,* if Virginia Woolf had conceived him as a comic figure, might easily have become another Walter Shandy. In *Orlando* the action of pages 159–169 takes "days," but it occurred, the reader is told, in "three and a half seconds"; elsewhere, it is winter and summer in the same scene. Like Sterne, Virginia Woolf distrusted factual knowledge, and used facts only as stepping-off places for imaginative perception of reality. In *Orlando,* a fantasy exploiting the comic values of irony, Virginia Woolf was able, not only to use Sterne's techniques for her purposes, but also to extend the meaning of her own book by reminding the reader of Sterne's.

Orlando, dealing as it does with the art and attitudes of four centuries in England, is a treasure house for anyone interested in Virginia Woolf's opinions. There can be seen, for example, her admiration of the Elizabethan age and contempt for the Victorian;[29] her concern for the position of women;[30] her theory that English literature, at some time during the seventeenth century, changed from "masculine" to "feminine," as well as her ideas about literature in general; her dislike of doctors,[31] of lecturers,[32] of popular society, and of professors, especially American professors. These, interesting though they are, have no primary significance for her art; but there are in *Orlando* certain statements about concepts vitally important in determining not only this novel but those that preceded and followed it as well.

This novel, for example, repeats and enlarges upon Proustian—ultimately Bergsonian—ideas of time and memory:

Time, unfortunately, though it makes animals and vegetables bloom and fade with amazing punctuality, has no such simple effect upon the mind of man. The mind of man, moreover, works with equal strangeness upon the body of time. An hour, once it lodges in the queer element of the human spirit, may be stretched to fifty or a hundred times its clock length; on the other hand, an hour may be accurately represented on the timepiece of the mind by one second. This extraordinary discrepancy between time on the clock and time in the mind is less known than it should be and deserves fuller investigation.

So it is that when Orlando is alone, "the seconds began to round and fill until it seemed as if they would never fall. They filled themselves, moreover, with the strangest variety of objects." This recalls Proust's famous assertion: "Une heure n'est pas qu'une heure, c'est un vase rempli de parfums, de sons, de projets et de climats. Ce que nous appelons la réalité est un certain rapport entre ces sensations et ces souvenirs qui nous entourent simultanément."[33] Orlando finds that every thing is more than itself. "Every single thing, once he tried to dislodge it from its place in his mind, he found thus encumbered with matter like the lump of glass which, after a year at the bottom of the sea, is grown about with bones and dragonflies, and coins and the tresses of drowned women." If he thinks of friendship or of truth, "his whole past, which seemed to him of extreme length and variety, rushed into the falling second, swelled it a dozen times its natural size, coloured it a thousand tints, and filled it with all the odds and ends in the universe." It is precisely this recovery of time past that the novel is to accomplish, and for which such passages as this prepare the reader. In Proustian fashion, it is the "fat, furred woman" whom the twentieth-century Orlando notices in the department store, and who reminds her of Sasha, who will give the first impetus to that complete recovery of the past and recognition of reality that constitutes the novel's catastrophe. In just the same way, Marcel of *À la Recherche du temps perdu* experiences a series of vague and elusive remembrances that puzzle him, but the true meaning and value of which he does not understand until his final perception of reality.

This network of concepts, although expressed with new materials and technique in *Orlando,* is of course essentially the same as it was in the preceding novels. But Virginia Woolf's concept of androgyneity is first given adequate expression in *Orlando.*

Basically, the theory of androgyneity is akin to Coleridge's: the best critics, he believed, are possessed of androgynous minds. Certainly the same can be said of novelists; the great novelist is able to characterize persons of the opposite sex as convincingly as those of his own. In her book *A Room of One's Own,* published the year after *Orlando,* Virginia Woolf classified authors according to this androgyneity. Noting that "neither Mr. Galsworthy nor Mr. Kipling has a spark of the woman in him. . . . They lack suggestive power," she went on to say that Milton, Ben Jonson, Wordsworth, and even Tolstoi are too much male; that Shelley is sexless; but that Shakespeare, Keats, Sterne, Cowper, Lamb, and Coleridge are androgynous. "Proust," she added, "was wholly androgynous, if not perhaps a little too much of a woman. But that failing is too rare for one to complain of it, since without some mixture of the kind the intellect seems to predominate and the other faculties of the mind harden and become barren."[34]

The mention of intellect indicates directly enough that this theory is not alien to the general "metaphysic" of Virginia Woolf's art. Mrs. Dalloway, Mrs. Ramsay, if they are to overleap the boundaries of their own individual selves, must arrive at an understanding of men as well as of women—sex cannot raise a barrier to cleave the basic likeness that they find. Further, they must embrace—and not exclude—intellect in this intuitive perception: to exclude is to separate. Bergson had spoken of intellect on the one hand and intuition on the other; so had Proust. But although intellect can never lead to intuition, intuition can lead to intellect; thus Mr. Ramsay is intellectual; Mrs. Ramsay, Clarissa Dalloway, and Terence Hewet are not only intuitive, but intellectual *and* intuitive. It follows that woman—as a symbol for intuitive knowledge—is different from man—as a symbol for intellectual knowledge—only insofar as she possesses two kinds of knowledge and not just one.

The germs of this theory, as it appears in *The Voyage Out,* have already been noticed. *Night and Day* also contains hints of it: Katharine is twice compared to Rosalind, and Katharine and Cassandra "represented very well the manly and the womanly sides of the feminine nature." In *Jacob's Room* the feeling of Bonamy for Jacob is the first occurrence of this androgyneity on a physical level in the novels. *Mrs. Dalloway* contains several suggestions of the theory: Peter Walsh is "attractive to women who liked the sense that he was not altogether manly"; Mrs. Dalloway once had an adolescent crush on Sally Seton, and was able, when she looked at other women, sometimes, "whether it was pity, or their beauty, or that she was older, or some accident—like a faint scent, or a violin next door" to "feel what men felt. Only for a moment; but it was enough. It was a sudden revelation." In *To the Lighthouse* there occurs the phrase, describing Mrs. Ramsay's daughters, "the manliness in their girlish hearts."

Most of these examples are mere hints, unimportant and un-convincing in themselves. In *Orlando,* however, since it was a fantasy, Virginia Woolf could develop this idea as imaginatively as she wished; and after she had articulated it in this novel, it became more important and significant to her, to judge from her later work. Androgyneity is found on a variety of levels in this book. It has already been noted that Orlando actually changes from man to woman; while she is a boy he is loved, not only by the Archduke Harry (as the Archduchess Harriet), but also by other men: "the adored of many women and some men." Orlando, to widen her experience, fell in love for a time with another woman; and she often changes her sex by changing her clothes. "She was man; she was woman; she knew the secrets, shared the weaknesses of each." This of course indicates Or-lando's ability to understand beyond the confinements of her sex as a human being and an artist. At first Orlando cannot de-cide whether she is happier as a woman than he was as a man; but she soon thinks of men with pity, and from the time of his transmogrification she becomes more and more woman, until finally she is a "real woman at last." In other words, Orlando, by becoming a woman, adds intuitive to intellectual knowledge, and the gradual development of that intuitive faculty leads her to her final perception of reality.

Virginia Woolf's concept of androgyneity is not that there is really no difference between men and women. Only by intuitive perception can men and women be the same; to be a woman, then, is in this sense to be as different as possible from a man— to know by intuition and intellect instead of by intellect alone.

The difference between the sexes is, happily, one of great profundity. Clothes are but a symbol of something hid deep beneath. It was a change in Orlando herself that dictated her choice of a woman's dress and of a woman's sex. And perhaps in this she was only expressing rather more openly than usual ... something that happens to most people without being thus plainly expressed. For here again, we come to a dilemma. Different though the sexes are, they intermix. In every human being a vacillation from one sex to the other takes place, and often it is only the clothes that keep the male or female likeness, while underneath the sex is the very opposite of what it is above.

For Proust, perversion was symbolic mainly of the state of the society he was depicting. For Virginia Woolf it was also used for symbolic value, but of a rather different kind. In her later novels there is a very sharp distinction drawn between empathetic androgyny and perversion. The latter is used to symbolize a pathetic inability to communicate—to throw off the limitations of self and of purely intellectual knowledge; the former is communication and assumption of the true self by means of intuitive as well as intellectual perception. Orlando can be at once the manly woman and womanly man— she can achieve a balance of intellect and intuition possible only in a fantasy; thus, before her complete perception of reality, she has become a "real woman," so that her final realization of herself transcends the fantastic. It is for this reason that her vision of truth—of the wild goose—is not possible until her husband (who drops from an airplane) joins her.

The mentally androgynous man and woman can understand each other with a perfection impossible to those barred behind the limitations of their sex. When Orlando and Marmaduke meet, they understand each other immediately:

An awful suspicion rushed into both their minds simultaneously.
"You're a woman, Shel!" she cried.
"You're a man, Orlando!" he cried.

The truth is that both are androgynous, that each is able to see beyond quantitative differentiation. To be only a man in mind or only a woman (when woman is fact not symbol) is to be hopelessly isolated and to perish. This is also clear, indeed, in the "Great Frost" scene, which is probably the most famous single passage in Virginia Woolf's writing. It has been widely praised as one of the greatest purple passages in English prose, and is constantly being reproduced.[85] Even here, in view of Virginia Woolf's use of water imagery, her mind as well as her fancy can be seen at work: when the river is frozen over, so is everything else—all is suspended, immobile, dead. Before the ice can thaw completely, great damage is done. This is exactly the situation at the conclusion of the novel: while Orlando is moving toward complete realization of herself, clock time (the striking of clocks) causes her to undergo a terrific shock—"her own body quivered and tingled as if suddenly stood naked in a hard frost." While she perceives pure-time duration, it is "as if her mind had become a fluid that flowed round things and enclosed them completely."

As an artist, Orlando "had a faith of her own" but "no traffic with the usual God." The "sins and imperfections" in her "spiritual state" are technical flaws in her poetry, and her divinity is the thought of that poetry. She has great admiration for the work of Sir Thomas Browne, although Nick Greene tells her that "as for Browne, he was for writing poetry in prose, and people soon got tired of such conceits as that." It is of Browne that Orlando thinks when, later in her life, "slowly there had opened within her something intricate and many-chambered, which one must take a torch to explore, in prose not verse."

It was—as her critical writing makes clear—with some such thought in mind that Virginia Woolf must have written her next novel, *The Waves.* According to some critics, *Orlando* seems not to be a "novel" in any rigid sense of that word; also according to them, *To the Lighthouse* is rather a poem than a novel. Still, it is in connection, not with these, but with *The Waves,* Virginia Woolf's furthest extension of the form of the novel proper, that her own ideas about novel form can best be examined, since they are her justification for even her most extreme innovations. *The Waves,* it becomes clear at once, is in every way an innovation.

In its external pattern *The Waves* seems simple enough. It is written in two types of prose: descriptive and dramatic. The descriptive sequence, printed in italics, is divided into ten brief sections. After each of the first eight of these descriptive sections there is a sequence of soliloquies, and after the ninth there is a single soliloquy which is by far the longest section of the book.

The descriptive parts depict a single day on an English beach (perhaps on the northeast coast) near the nursery school that is the place setting for the first section of soliloquies. The first of these descriptive passages is portrayed from the shore at dawn; but in the later passages, as the sun moves higher, the perspective changes so that at noon the reader looks with the sun upon the whole of Great Britain and parts of France, Spain, and Africa, as well as upon the sea; the scope gradually decreases again as the sun sets. Furthermore, the time of a year is described and passes concurrently with the time of day—in the morning it is spring; at noon, summer; and so on—and the time of day and year in each section coincides with the ages of the speakers in the following section of soliloquies—at dawn, they are children; in the early morning, adolescents; and so on. There is, however, no connection between the time settings here and those in the dramatic sequences, or of course between the place settings after the first dramatic section. The descriptive part of the book can be read by itself as an artistic whole, but actually its more complex and symbolic significance becomes fully apparent only through the dramatic part. Similarly, the dramatic sections constitute a whole in themselves, but complete understanding of them depends in part upon recognition of their constant references, direct and indirect, to the descriptive sections.

The soliloquies of six persons—Bernard, Susan, Neville, Jinny, Louis, and Rhoda—constitute the dramatic sequences of *The Waves*. These dramatic sections have definite place settings but not always definite time settings. Although the six characters are very different from one another, they can be divided into three compatible duos: Bernard and Susan are alike in their natural fulfillment, though his is a mental and hers a physical fulfillment; Neville and Jinny are alike in their unnatural fufillment and romanticism; and Louis and Rhoda are alike in their refusal to be fulfilled—in their fear of life. It follows that the six persons can also be divided into three pairs of opposites. However great their differences, these characters are the same in one way: all of them are asking questions about the meaning of life and experience. None of them—although Jinny comes close to being an exception—is content with a day-to-day living regulated by the social standards and patterns that can so easily drown out their questions. The foil for all of them, therefore, is Percival, whom they all love and envy. Percival is seen only indirectly: he has no soliloquies, because he is not one of the questioning minority with whom Virginia Woolf is concerned in this book. Percival is pure action, and not action mixed with various amounts of reflection like the six soliloquizers; he does not ask why he is alive or they are—he simply lives. For all of them there is something refreshing and healthful in Percival, whose sudden, meaningless death is therefore the climax of the book, since it reminds them of the other half of a hidden pattern, one half of which they believed they had almost succeeded in tracing. From this climax there develops a double catastrophe: the suicide of Rhoda, and the final soliloquy in which Bernard recapitulates what has gone before and brings the whole problem to the solution that, as will be seen, the descriptive sequence has postulated.

The soliloquies are not of course to be considered as spoken by the characters—those of the children in the first dramatic sequence are ample proof of this:

"I see a ring," said Bernard, "hanging above me. It quivers and hangs in a loop of light."

"I see a slab of pale yellow," said Susan, "spreading away until it meets a purple stripe."

"I hear a sound," said Rhoda, "cheep, chirp; cheep, chirp; going up and down."

"I see a globe," said Neville, "hanging down in a drop against the enormous flanks of some hill."

"I see a crimson tassel," said Jinny, "twisted with gold threads."

"I hear something stamping," said Louis. "A great beast's foot is chained. It stamps, and stamps, and stamps."

Again, the perfect order of these soliloquies and the duologue form they sometimes assume, as well as the inner order of each, show that they are not to be considered as stream-of-consciousness monologues. Rather, these soliloquies are transcriptions of the feelings, perceptions, and thoughts of six persons by a central intelligence—that of the author. Although the passages are projected in dramatic fashion, the point of view is omniscient—one person is arranging and telling everything. Thus, in spite of the fact that the reader moves from one personality to another, and follows these personalities from childhood to old age, he is constantly restrained, by the very prose style in which they are written, from imagining the soliloquies to be the words, thoughts, or streams of consciousness of the speakers themselves. This style does not adapt itself to the personalities of the various speakers, but remains inflexible, even though it is impossible to think of the flamboyant Jinny as actually speaking or thinking with the same vocabulary and syntax employed by, say, the shy and scholarly Louis. This uniformity of style in the soliloquies has several functions, one of the most important of which is that it emphasizes and extends the book's statement that the very unity found beneath diversity is the essence of the diversity itself—that life's flux is precisely its unity.

Perhaps the germ of this soliloquy method is the beginning of the second part of *To the Lighthouse:*

"Well, we must wait for the future to show," said Mr. Bankes, coming in from the terrace.

"It's almost too dark to see," said Andrew, coming up from the beach.

"One can hardly tell which is the sea and which is the land," said Prue.

"Do we leave that light burning?" said Lily as they took their coats off indoors.

Here, however, the characters are really speaking to each other, and what they are doing as they speak is recorded in the conventional manner. In *The Waves* all that exists outside the monologues is an indication of who is speaking: "said Bernard... said Rhoda," and so on. For the reader nothing *happens* outside the soliloquies; all action is refracted through the speeches themselves: " 'Now we march, two by two,' said Louis, 'orderly, processional, into chapel. I like the dimness that falls as we enter the sacred building. I like the orderly progress.' " In this way nothing simply happens; everything happens in a special way for each of the speakers. Louis likes the chapel and its order, but Neville detests them; there is, therefore, no objective account of what goes on in the chapel, but only accounts colored by the individual speaker's attitude. Nothing is simply one thing. This idea, which was stated in *To the Lighthouse* and *Orlando,* is shown formally without being explicitly stated in *The Waves;* more than ever the form of this book manages to express its meaning directly.

If nothing is simply one thing, neither is any of these characters one person. Each is differentiated from the others by his name and attitude, but each speaks with a common language and style. Bernard can say: " 'What I call "my life," it is not one life that I look back upon; I am not one person; I am many people; I do not altogether know who I am—Jinny, Susan, Neville, Rhoda, or Louis: or how to distinguish my life from theirs.... For this is not one life; nor do I always know if I am man or woman, Bernard or Neville, Louis, Susan, Jinny or Rhoda—so strange is the contact of one with another.' " Paradoxically, if none of these characters by himself is one person, nevertheless all of them merge to form a single identity, just as

Orlando's selves had done, in a "communication." But, again as in *Orlando,* this unity is itself an essential diversity rather than a common denominator.

Bergson had said that although a person can go from intuition to intellect, he can never go from intellect to intuition. *The Waves* is a demonstration of the futility of intellectual analysis by itself and of the validity of intuitional perception. By means of the intellect, each person sees himself as single, separate, and isolated; by means of intuition, however, he becomes at once infinitely divisible within himself and one with all that exists.

The first sequence of soliloquies presents the direct acquaintance of children with this dualism. Bernard, sitting with Susan, says: " 'When we sit together, close ... we melt into each other with phrases. We are edged with mist. We make an unsubstantial territory.' " But when Mrs. Constable gives Bernard his bath and squeezes a water-filled sponge over him, the sensation gives him an individual identity: " 'I am covered with warm flesh.' " Physically, Bernard is only one person; mentally, he is not. Proust said: "Avoir un corps c'est la grande menace pour l'esprit. ... le corps enferme l'esprit dans une forteresse";[36] Bernard, much later in his life, says: " 'Sometimes indeed, when I pass a cottage with a light in the window where a child has been born, I could implore them not to squeeze the sponge over that new body.' " This is, of course, the same dualism found in "Kew Gardens" and the earlier novels. The flame-candle antithesis is here a spirit-matter antithesis: words, a manifestation of spirit, can produce unity; flesh, a manifestation of matter, insists upon separateness. The intellect perceives matter; the intuition, spirit. This first section is remarkable as a description of children's immediate relationship with life and their direct apprehension of it. Bernard is here never aware of a conflict between one and many: he simply receives impressions, and it is the nature, not of the impressions, but of his reception, that Virginia Woolf defines. The reader does not know, for example, until much later in the book that what Bernard saw as " 'a ring ... hanging above me. It quivers and hangs in a loop of light,' " was actually the knob of a drawer.

So it is with the other children. Jinny, who is to go through life having one love affair after another, suddenly kisses Louis on the nape of the neck. This causes Susan—who is to be "glutted with natural happiness" as the mother of a large family—to become violently angry and jealous. Neville, who is to go through life searching for happiness with some one other man, cannot appreciate Bernard's sympathy for Susan; and he thinks only that, by running away to comfort her, Bernard has stolen the knife with which he and Neville had been carving a boat. Rhoda and Louis, always to be lonely, are shown as lonely children. Rhoda is pathetic in her desire to escape from herself—a desire that leads her finally to suicide. Louis is equally pathetic in his belief that the whole world is himself; he is later to impose his own sense of order upon others, just as Sir William Bradshaw had done in *Mrs. Dalloway*. Louis differs from Bernard insofar as, instead of surrendering his identity, he attempts to stamp that identity absolutely upon all with which he comes into contact.

The second dramatic section is concerned with these characters' awareness of life and attempt to define it. They are shown at school. To the extent to which they define intellectually, they are never able—nor will they be throughout the book—to achieve a satisfactory solution. Bernard, the phrase maker, attempts to separate one person from another and to put into words each person's individuality; he cannot succeed. But in a moment of perception he realizes intuitively that " 'we are not single, we are one,' " without, however, grasping the significance of this realization. The others, meanwhile, continue to insist upon their separate identities, and to refuse sacrifice of their separateness. When Neville's train draws into the London station, he says:

"I will let the others get out before me. I will sit one moment before

I emerge into that chaos, that tumult. I will not anticipate what is to come. The huge uproar is in my ears. It sounds and resounds under this glass roof like the surge of a sea. We are cast down on the platform with our handbags. We are whirled asunder. My sense of self almost perishes; my contempt. I become drawn in, tossed down, thrown sky-high. I step out on to the platform, grasping tightly all that I possess—one bag."

The glass roof is container and soundboard for the chaotic, vital surge of "life itself." The identification of Neville with a wave is not an isolated use of this metaphor, which of course occurs for all the characters throughout the book. This image is sufficiently obvious to convey its meaning, with any number of modifications, and yet never to distract attention: the individual life is a wave, and life itself the sea; to look at oneself as only one wave is to perish when that single wave breaks, but to see oneself as an indivisible part of the sea, composed of innumerable drops of water—as part of wave after wave—is to gain immortality. This, as will be seen, is the nature of Bernard's final and complete realization. Moreover, Virginia Woolf has made of the novel itself a "glass roof": a construct to cover and discover the unity, endlessness, infinite diversity of human awareness and to focus the spectacle beneath immediate light so that spectacle and light are achieved as a single, disciplined form.

The third dramatic section describes the thoughts of the six speakers a few years later. At college Bernard is beset with the problem of his own identity, a central problem in this section. " 'I am not one and simple, but complex and many,' " he thinks; and yet " 'underneath ... I am ... integrated.' " He is unable to solve this problem of complexity: his "true self" is dissatisfied with some of the antics of his many selves, but he cannot define his true self; he knows only that precisely when he is most diverse he is also most individual. Neville too asks, " 'Who am I?' " He is at one moment a great poet; at the next, Bernard. Bernard can comprehend Neville, and Neville can comprehend Bernard; but neither can comprehend himself. Bernard realizes that he is separate and one when he is with Neville but many when he is by himself. Yet this individuality of the social self is merely appearance. Louis, now a businessman, also searches for his true self. " 'I am conscious of flux, of disorder; of annihilation and despair. If this is all, this is worthless,' " he thinks, ironically unable to realize the positive nature of flux and "disorder." He decides that " 'I will reduce you to order,' " and so begins his superimposition of an arbitrary and alien order upon the mobility of life. For the girls the problem is the same. They too make the mistake of confusing appearance with reality: of clinging to their social selves and denying the validity of the manyness apparent to them in privacy. With the others Rhoda decides that in love there is " 'a world immune from change.' " Love, they think, will give their lives stability.

This belief is tested and found seemingly true in the fourth dramatic section. The six meet at a restaurant where they have gathered to give Percival—with whom each of them is, in his own way, in love—a farewell dinner: he is leaving for India. Percival himself is, naturally enough, in love with Susan. At the end of this dinner the six soliloquizers are completely happy. They now believe that their social pact, founded upon a common love for Percival—the life of action and behavior, rather than of thought and being—allows them to " 'issue from the darkness of solitude' " into a real and communal unity: " 'sitting together now we love each other and believe in our own endurance.' " For a moment they have succeeded in transcending the flux within them and without, and they believe that this moment will last. " 'We are creators. We too have made something that will join the innumerable congregations of past time. We too, as we put on our hats and push open the door, stride not into chaos, but into a world that our own force can subjugate and make part of the illumined and everlasting road.' "

Then Percival dies. Chaos is reëstablished. Much as in *To the Lighthouse,* a seeming truth has been proved false. Here, however, it is not time so much as chance and essential meaninglessness that destroys the unity. Here again the truth has not been the whole truth: the six characters have transcended flux, not in "pure-time duration," but in an allegiance to the apparent oneness of their social selves; they have forced the moment of unity instead of simply accepting true unity. Therefore the unity is an intellectualized creation that cannot endure. Percival's death—he has been thrown from a horse—makes life once more chaotic. Bernard tries to understand Percival's death in its relation to the birth of his son, which occurred at the same time. He thinks it now obvious that life has no order; troubled, he enters an art gallery to attempt escape from " 'the sequence ... the usual order' " of clock time. He sees that Percival, who stayed always within the sequence, was the opposite of him and of the artists who have " 'minds like mine outside the sequence.' " After realizing this much, he returns to the sequence of social life, refusing to worry the problem any longer. Rhoda, on the other hand, goes shopping in Oxford Street, seeking a bond between everyday actions and Percival's death. Finally in despair she decides that the order of art and of organized life is at once man's redemption and his excuse. It is precisely this acceptance of human organization that Percival's death has made impossible for Bernard. The two—Bernard and Rhoda—thus cross each other at the climax of the book: she moving, as it were, to the surface, and he to the basis and all-embracing meaning of life.

In the sixth dramatic section—a very short one—the lives of the six characters have all become patterned. Louis is a successful businessman, operating a steamship company, spreading order: " 'I have fused my many lives into one; I have helped by my assiduity and decision to score those lines on the map there by which the different parts of the world are laced together.... I press on, from chaos making order' "; but actually he is imposing a false order, becoming more and more certain that his lines drawn on the map are justified by the map itself. Susan has married, and now thinks only of her children; she, like Bernard, will find immortality, but hers will be the physical immortality of her children and children's children. Jinny, now past thirty, still flits from party to party, from one romance to another. Neville, pursuing his unnatural happiness, is in constant fear of desertion; and, though he is now a great poet, he is torn between perfection and the wildness that he cannot share. Like Jinny, he is a romantic, going from one person to another in a search for "the one" and confusing each new lover with love itself. As a man, Neville is unnatural in his perversion—a symbol of his refusal to surrender his identity—just as Jinny, as a woman, is unnatural in her romanticistic search, which keeps her from marriage and motherhood: her refusal to assume her immortal identity as Susan has assumed hers.

The seventh dramatic section presents the consequences of the patterns that all the characters except Bernard have imposed upon their lives by refusing to reach beyond their individual separateness. For even Susan, although she has fulfilled herself perfectly, has made one mistake: "'My son,' I say, 'My daughter,'" and "'I possess all I see.'" Somewhat like Louis when he was a child, Susan has insisted too much upon her *possession* of what surrounds her, and by doing so has failed to attain more than physical immortality. Mrs. Ramsay, like Bernard, could attain both physical and spiritual immortality; but Mrs. Ramsay saw others in herself rather than herself in others. Susan is always unhappy when she thinks of Jinny, for despite her own happiness she envies Jinny's good times. If she could transcend clock time and space completely, however, Susan would lose her separateness, become Jinny as well as Susan, and be a part of all experience. Jinny herself, growing old, realizes that soon her beauty will be gone and she will no longer excite attention, but she goes on living the life she has made for herself: she, more

than any other of the six, illustrates the physical results of the
passing of time. Neville refuses any longer to seek a reason for
life, but clutches at love as an escape from having to face the
problem. Louis, for all his order and success, is still seeking to
" 'make reason of it all.' " Rhoda, in Spain, is filled with dread of
life and hatred of human beings. Each of these five persons is
discontent with the pattern of his life; only Bernard, who has
constantly refused to impose a pattern, is still hopeful of finding
" 'a final statement.' " He has gone for ten days to Rome; there,
still unsure of the purpose of life, he decides that at any rate the
order of religion is a false one: " 'In these dilemmas the devout
consult those violet-sashed and sensual-looking gentry who are
trooping past me. But for ourselves, we resent teachers. Let a
man get up and say, "Behold, this is the truth," and instantly I
perceive a sandy cat filching a piece of fish in the background.
Look, you have forgotten the cat, I say.' "

The eighth dramatic section is occasioned by a final reunion
of the six friends at the Inn at Hampton Court, arranged by
Bernard. Although these people are now middle-aged none of
them has been able to form a conclusion about life and experience, and yet each believes the others to have found one. To
Bernard life now seems an arrangement of patterns in the midst
of a flux. Neville attempts to impress Susan, wishing to make
the identity of another person " 'crouch beneath one's own.' "
Susan, on the other hand, must discredit Neville in order to be
herself; she finds herself by subtracting it from him. Jinny, despite her age, is sure of having been right in her attitude toward
life, and is unafraid. Louis, although he is happiest alone, says
that he would nevertheless follow his friends to the death;
though he condemns them, he loves them. Rhoda, miserable at
having to appear in public, is now conscious of a vague but pierc-
ing doom ahead of her. It is difficult, Bernard thinks, for the six
friends to be together now, for life has built walls between them;
but, he thinks, they no longer draw comparisons and distinc-

tions. "'And we ourselves,'" he says, "'walking six abreast, what do we oppose, with this random flicker of light in us that we call brain and feeling, how can we do battle against this flood; what has permanence? Our lives too stream away, down the unlighted avenues, past the strip of time, unidentified.'" He had once a hazy perception of immortality; it has gone. For a moment the six look at the totality of their lives, and then that totality is over. Mutability and undulation have won over any attempts to halt and organize them: this is all the six lives can prove. The "sequence" has triumphed; the concatenation of "musts" in life is the only answer to questions about life. Bernard decides that he is one and indivisible in himself. The "flame" has now been reduced to a "flicker"; the only truth is the truth of separate, spatialized, material identity.

The ninth and final dramatic section of *The Waves,* a long monologue by Bernard, most of which takes the form of a speech to a stranger whom he has met one evening in a restaurant, is for the most part devoted to an intellectual analysis of his past life. He is an old man now, bent upon explaining the meaning of his life. This analysis takes Bernard from one pole of the matter-spirit dichotomy to the other and back again. All, he begins by saying, is flux; everything that happens, however minute, lasts forever, but it affects each person differently— calling forth different responses, forming different patterns— and the separation of individuals causes suffering. Percival was the unphilosophical, unquestioning leader of men, who would have "'done justice.... No lullaby has ever occurred to me capable of singing him to rest.'" Each person can realize only certain segments of life, and so is envious of others, no matter how fulfilled himself. Bernard, however, liking those who differ from him, who do not question life, joins them; and his mold of separateness is gradually loosened—he is completely merged in his experiences. A person must reach outside his own experience, to the symbolic, which is perhaps the only permanence.

(Thus, during the entire book, the characters have expressed themselves in terms of the symbolism of the descriptive sections.) " 'The tree alone resisted our eternal flux,' " but Bernard became one person after another, and found his own self only by looking at the tree—always the same, although each of his friends was so different. He thus became the inheritor of the past and its continuer.

Social order, he goes on, though deep in itself, is only a surface lie above the flux. Life is not a solid, to be turned and studied. He had found enough, however, in the surface of life—the conventional ordering and purposing—until Percival's death entered the picture as an antithesis to his son's birth. The stability of things in themselves, of art, gave him momentary freedom, but he could not ignore the gap between life and death: precautions are taken to keep alive, and yet death overrides them. All seemed meaningless. First came hatred and the wish to fight, then contentment again with the sequence. But in a moment of insight he is able to say, " 'The true order of things—this is our perpetual illusion—is now apparent.' " Bernard sought out Neville and found companionship and silent order, but Neville began to wait for someone else, deserting to another world. Thus Bernard is unknown to his friends, and they are unknown to him. Yet his life is theirs too, and he is each of them and indistinguishable from them: he cannot separate " 'my life.' " At Hampton, for a moment, order came; all of them were one. " 'The moment was all; the moment was enough.' " But then Bernard could not distinguish his own identity.

He became despondent of the flux: his notebooks, in which he had tried to write phrases that would capture something outside the sequence, had recorded only changes. Then for a moment, seeing the world without a self, he found the truth. He repeats that he does not know if he is all his friends or one and distinct. The living and the dead, he says, are divided, but there is no wall of division between them. What matters is to lose the illusion of personal identity.

He is now " 'immeasurably receptive,' " and without desire or curiosity, and now completely within himself—one old man; now all is order, now all disorder.

At this point in his monologue Bernard is left alone by his companion. The flux stops. He throws away his book of phrases, because words cannot explain anything: he needs " 'a howl; a cry,' " the language of children. But the sequence pursues him: he "must" leave the restaurant, for it is closing time.

Here Bernard's intellectual analysis ends. It has been a confused, irresolute, undecisive probing of his past experience, filled with contradictions and vacillations, able to sort and separate, but not to distinguish truth from falsity, reality from appearance; Bernard has spatialized the facts of his life, but has been unable to organize them into any lasting pattern. Neither has any of the other characters, except one: Rhoda has committed suicide. But her suicide is much different from Septimus' in its meaning. Rhoda had placed her faith in the surface order of life, and that had failed her: her suicide was, then, not a "plunge" into life, but a retreat to the core of her own isolated selfhood, very like the death of Rachel Vinrace in *The Voyage Out*.

Bernard now emerges from the restaurant and stands in the street. It is the verge of dawn; but Bernard at first derides dawn as a mere step in the sequence. In phrases taken from the descriptive section of the book, the beginning of the dawn is pictured. This description creates a transition between clock time and mind time, between the sequence and pure duration; Bernard moves from it to his final and complete perception of reality, in which he achieves a sympathy for his opposite, Percival, and in which he is able to see "spirit" as a reality embracing "flesh"; intuition tells him what intellect could not—that the undulation itself is order.

"Another general awakening. The stars draw back and are extinguished. The bars deepen themselves between the waves. The film of mist thickens on the fields. A redness gathers on the roses, even on the pale rose that hangs by the bedroom window. A bird chirps. Cottagers light their early candles. Yes, this is the eternal renewal, the incessant rise and fall and fall and rise again.

"And in me too the wave rises. It swells; it arches its back. I am aware once more of a new desire, something rising beneath me like a proud horse whose rider first spurs and then pulls him back. What enemy do we now perceive advancing against us, you whom I ride now, as we stand pawing this stretch of pavement? It is death. Death is the enemy. It is death against whom I ride with my spear couched and my hair flying back like a young man's, like Percival's, when he galloped in India. I strike spurs into my horse. Against you I will fling myself, unvanquished and unyielding, O Death!"

There is a remarkable analogy between this final passage of *The Waves* and one of Bergson's most famous passages from *Creative Evolution:* "All the living hold together, and all yield to the same tremendous push. The animal takes its stand on the plant, man bestrides animality, and the whole of humanity, in space and in time, is one immense army galloping before and beside and behind each of us in an overwhelming charge able to beat down every resistance and clear the most formidable obstacles, perhaps even death."[37]

After Bernard's final speech, however, there is one more sentence, concluding the descriptive sequence and the book as a whole: *"The waves broke on the shore."* Critics usually take this to mean Bernard's death; critics who find *The Waves* a pessimistic book believe the sentence to mean also that Bernard's final vision was illusory and false.[38] Such an interpretation seems of doubtful value. Certainly Bernard would not have believed himself physically immortal except in his children—but this sentence is not in a minor key. All through the descriptive sequence, even in the part describing the dawn, waves have broken against the shore. Of course, from one point of view—for which matter was the only reality—the breaking of the wave would mean Bernard's death and the falsity of his final perception. But there is a passage, earlier in Bernard's final summing up, that reveals the meaning of this concluding sentence:

"It is strange how force ebbs away and away into some dry creek. Sitting alone, it seems we are spent; our waters can only just surround feebly that spike of sea-holly; we cannot reach that further pebble so as to wet it. It is over, we are ended. But wait—I sat all night waiting—an impulse again runs through us; we rise, we toss back a mane of white spray; we pound on the shore; we are not to be confined."

Here Bernard goes on to say that this is the sequence. At the conclusion, however, when the same metaphor is repeated, he has realized that this is life itself: he has embraced his opposite—his own pure-time existence transcending Percival's clock-time existence—and gained immortality. The rock, the shore, in Bergsonian language would be matter; the wave would be a vital impetus raging against matter—immobility, death—in a never ending undulation; it is in this sense that the waves break on the shore at the conclusion of *The Waves*. Bernard's apprehension of reality is, as the imagery with which he states it shows, symbolized throughout the book by the descriptive sections; there, as in Bernard's final speech, the waves symbolize an impetus common to all life—nothing new in Virginia Woolf's work—and of which each individual is a carrier; they are at once life and life's justification. Bernard's final realization that life's flux is its unity creates a harmony between his statement about life and the statement made in the descriptive sequence; further, just as individuals are used by the sea of flux in its constant becoming, so the individuals of the book are used by its central intelligence as a means for this realization. Thus the descriptive sections are a symbolic statement of the truth toward which the whole dramatic part is moving, and which Bernard finally discovers. Through the descriptive sections, the interdependent symbolism, and the statements of the characters, the reader has this truth constantly before him, though he realizes it, with Bernard, only at the catastrophe. Because of this, the conclusion is particularly satisfying: the reader has an illusion of confirming, from his "own experience," Bernard's statement. The answer has never been given in terms with which he can cope logically, or in terms that arouse his reason. Everything has been done with seemingly innocent description and conventional imagery, the latent meaning coming only as an affirmation by the reader of Bernard's answer to the problem.

Virginia Woolf has been accused of writing mere impressionistic rhapsody in the descriptive section of *The Waves*. Philip Toynbee, discussing the book, actually dismisses this portion with a footnote: "I have said nothing of the intermediary passages of prose-poetry. They are clearly decoration, and irrelevant to this discussion."[39] Not only the descriptive section, but the book as a whole, has been subjected to a series of interesting but unsatisfactory interpretations that cause it to be perhaps the least understood of Virginia Woolf's works. Burgum called the waves a symbol of chaos and illusoriness;[40] W. H. Mellers wrote: "Our lives are shrouded in obscurity, and knowing nothing we turn on our wistfullest smiles and tread our way to the grave. It is difficult to see how an honest reader can discover any more 'profundity' in *The Waves* than this"[41]—difficult perhaps, but certainly worth the difficulty. For N. Elizabeth Monroe the book has no "central idea or mood."[42] D. S. Savage considers the book a "virtual surrender to meaninglessness," and offers Bernard's final summing up as evidence.[43] Gerald Sykes, reviewing *The Waves* when it first appeared, wrote that it was an example of "tea-room modernism," and that "anyone will perceive that the matter did not necessitate the form,"[44] although his review considered the form per se—as though form were a box to hold matter—and said nothing about the meaning. Dorothy Hoare, saying that there are no "beliefs" in the book, adds that it bears comparison with *The Waste Land,* and indicates allusions to Eliot's poetry;[45] F. L. Overcarsh goes so far as to call it "in certain respects a prose version of *The Waste Land*."[46] These statements are perhaps the result of the critics' having confused Bernard's intellectual analysis with his intuitive perception, although there seems to be no reason for such a confusion. On the other hand, some of Virginia Woolf's critics praise *The Waves* for what may be equally suspicious reasons: Deborah Newton says little to justify her calling the book Virginia Woolf's "supreme triumph";[47] and Bernard Blackstone, another admirer, writes: "What is Mrs. Woolf trying to do in this first section of *The Waves*? She is still pursuing her search for value.... She shows us that [the world] is all under the stress of an inexorable destiny."[48] But surely *The Waves* affirms value that Virginia Woolf had already found, and succeeded in communicating. The nature of that value is such that free will, not "destiny," is what Virginia Woolf shows us, although *The Waves* does not concern itself with this problem, which is dealt with explicitly in *Between the Acts*.

Of the accusations made against *The Waves*, perhaps the most frequent is that this book cannot be called a novel. As has been said, others of Virginia Woolf's books have also been criticized on this basis, but *The Waves*, differing as it does most obviously of them all from the conventional novel, has had to bear the brunt of the attack—"attack," because most critics who say that these books are not novels also say, or assume, that they are therefore unsuccessful.[49] This study is no attempt to decide the matter one way or another, but only to understand Virginia Woolf's work. Since, however, Virginia Woolf's own attitude toward prose fiction can be seen at once as a statement of intention and a justification for the form of her books, a brief examination of that attitude is relevant to an understanding of her work.

"The novel ... is a perpetual quest for reality, the field of its research being always the social world, the material of its analysis being always manners as the indication of the direction of man's soul."[50] According to this well-known definition by Lionel Trilling, *The Waves* is almost certainly not a novel; the characters of *The Waves* are not examined as they appear within a social structure—the author is not concerned with manners as images. A society, and a complex of social classes, had always been part and parcel of the novel form; in this complex the movement of individuals had taken certain patterns called plots. *The Waves* is partly about society—public behavior—but is not made of society; the six speakers exist primarily and directly as individuals ranged against a cosmic rather than a limited social background; indeed, manners are explicitly denied as means by which the artist can illumine his vision. *The Waves* is called, therefore, either a "lyric novel"[51] or simply a poem.

In her essay "The Niece of an Earl" Virginia Woolf discussed the dependence of the English novel upon a class complex. "In another century or so," the essay concludes, "none of these distinctions may hold good.... But what will happen to English fiction when it has come to pass that there are neither Generals, nieces, Earls, nor coats, we cannot imagine. It may change its character so that we no longer know it. It may become extinct. Novels may be written as seldom and as unsuccessfully by our descendants as the poetic drama by ourselves. The art of a truly democratic age will be—what?"[52] In *A Room of One's Own* she recognizes that such a book as *The Waves* is not properly to be called a novel: " 'The novel' (I give it inverted commas to mark my sense of the words' inadequacy), who shall say that even this most pliable of all forms is rightly shaped for [a woman's] use?" A woman author will provide "some new vehicle, not necessarily in verse, for the poetry in her."[53] More emphatically she wrote that if the novel depends entirely upon manners, novels will lose much of their greatness as manners change:

The process of discovery goes on perpetually. Always more of life is being reclaimed and recognized. Therefore, to fix the character of the novel, which is the youngest and most vigorous of the arts, at this moment would be like fixing the character of poetry in the Eighteenth Century and saying that because Gray's *Elegy* was "poetry" *Don*

Juan was impossible.... "the novel," as we still call it with such par-
simony of language, is already splitting apart into books which have
nothing in common but this inadequate title. Already the novelists
are so far apart that they scarcely communicate, and to one novelist
the work of another is quite genuinely unintelligible or quite genuinely negligible....

The novel, it is agreed, can follow life; it can amass details. But can
it also select? Can it symbolize? Can it give us an epitome as well as
an inventory? It was some such function as this that poetry dis-
charged in the past. But, whether for the moment or for some longer
time, poetry with her rhythms, her poetic diction, her strong flavour
of tradition, is too far from us today to do for us what she did for our
parents. Prose perhaps is the instrument best fitted to the complexity
and difficulty of modern life. And prose ... is still so youthful that we
scarcely know what powers it may not hold concealed within it. Thus
it is possible that the novel will come to differ as widely from the
novel of Tolstoy and Jane Austen as the poetry of Browning and
Byron differs from the poetry of Lydgate and Spenser.[54]

Here, Virginia Woolf is certainly using "novel" in its loosest
sense—simply as a word for "prose fiction"; if "novel" is used to
mean one *kind* of prose fiction, it cannot be used with so general
a term as "poetry." Given her sense of the word, Virginia Woolf
is at once both correct and uninteresting. However, she would
have thought it perhaps incorrect and uninteresting to confuse
a descriptive with a value judgment—to valuate by classifying
as do those who complain, instead of merely noting, that *The
Waves* is no novel in a precise sense of the word. Tolstoi himself,
in a conversation translated by Virginia Woolf in 1923, had said:

"I think that every great artist necessarily creates his own form also.
If the content of works of art can be infinitely varied, so also can their
form. Once Turgenev and I ... discussed this. He completely agreed
with me. We recalled all that is best in Russian literature and it
seemed that in these works the form was perfectly original. Omitting
Pushkin, let us take Gogol's *Dead Souls*. What is it? Neither a novel
nor a story. It is a something perfectly original."[55]

For Virginia Woolf, then, the novel was still in process of formation, and could not be called any one thing.

The Waves is, in Virginia Woolf's vocabulary, a "novel" but not a novel. Bernard himself, let it be noted, is a novelist. From his childhood he has been fascinated with phrases, and in school he begins to keep the notebook in which he records phrases that seem to capture the evanescent but lastingly significant incidents of his experience, thus hoping to rescue them from the flux. Furthermore, he enjoys telling stories to himself and to his companions, even as a child. But none of his stories is satisfactory. Often the members of his audience lose interest at the end of a story that has enthralled them during its progress; and it is with the conclusions of his stories that Bernard is most dissatisfied. All through his life he searches for *the* story, the one story that is merely suggested and distorted in all the other stories. At times he is convinced that his phrases are worthless, that there is no story to tell. Finally, just before his complete perception, he throws away his book of phrases, thinking that he has recorded not permanence but merely the very flux they were meant to stabilize. There is a story, he feels, but his phrases cannot tell it. Yet the truth for which Bernard has been searching as a human being, and which he finds and recognizes at the conclusion of the book, is also the story for which he has been searching as a novelist. It is of course the story told by *The Waves*.

"At the present moment," Virginia Woolf wrote in 1923, "we are suffering, not from decay, but from having no code of manners which writers and readers accept as a prelude to the more exciting intercourse of friendship."[56] It is a commonplace that the novelist of today cannot rely upon that general body of assumptions about life that enabled earlier authors to take for granted certain of the responses of their readers. A novelist, especially one who wishes to embrace and reach beyond—or perhaps even to question the validity of—society as an adequate symbol for human experience, must take for granted a body of assumptions that will justify the probability of the characters of his novel for only a minority of readers; or he must weave into the pattern of the novel itself the assumptions that justify the probability of what it has to say in such a way that the reader's own assumptions will not be called upon either to affirm or to deny—at least until he has finished the book—the validity of its statement. In other words, such a book must in some way furnish its own proof of what it says, and not depend upon the reader for affirmation of anything but the results. In *The Waves* the descriptive sequence makes possible a constant precipitating of justification from the solution in which the characters think and behave. The main structural difficulty that faced Virginia Woolf in writing this book, then, she solved in such a way that it became perhaps the main structural success. Her success may surely have been less limited, more triumphant, in her last works, which are all this as well as "novels" in the critical sense of the word. If the word "novel" is to be used precisely, critically, *The Waves* is not a novel; but *The Waves* is just about all that it set out to be: it is a work of art in which subject justifies form and form intends subject.

Virginia Woolf has been called by R. L. Chambers *"par excellence* the novelist of the Nineteen-Twenties." Three assumptions, according to Chambers, governed the period: that man is not a special creation; that time, space, and the universe are best seen as states of mind; that the individual is a complex of consciousness. It was, further, a time of postwar valuation, of the "lost generation," of escapism and of artists; its significant thinkers were Eliot, Lawrence, Virginia Woolf, and Aldous Huxley. Lawrence and Huxley, Chambers continues, are unlike Virginia Woolf in their denial of man's dignity; Virginia Woolf is the only technical innovator among them, though she is the least revolutionary thinker.[57]

Although several of these remarks are, to say the least, questionable, they nevertheless serve to suggest Virginia Woolf's place in the decade just after which she published *The Waves*. Huxley, Lawrence, and Virginia Woolf were the "big names of the years 1919–1929," says F. C. Frierson, adding that there was a decline in their influence from 1929 to 1940, "although reflections of their work are present."[58] Hugh Walpole wrote, in 1934, that Joyce, Lawrence, Virginia Woolf, and Huxley "have been [the] supreme influences on the English novel in the last ten years."[59]

Her contemporaries, as has been said, faced a problem very similar to Virginia Woolf's, although each set about solving it somewhat differently. Thus Aldous Huxley moved from the relativistic negativity of such novels as *Crome Yellow* (1921) to an absolutistic quasi mysticism based partly on the Vedas in *Eyeless in Gaza* (1936) and *Time Must Have a Stop* (1948). But—with the glowing exception of *Antic Hay* (1923)—Huxley's novels early and late are propagandistic vehicles rather than works of art; even *Point Counter Point* is burdened with some lumps of residual meaning—pure preaching—in "Philip Quarles's Notebooks." Despite his considerable talents, particularly for dialogue, Huxley's development is much more intellectual than artistic: his art is almost always a means rather than an end.

This cannot be said of D. H. Lawrence. Lawrence, who died in 1930—one year before the publication of *The Waves*—was first and foremost an artist, a great artist, whose thinking, like Virginia Woolf's, was intended always to be for art and not only through art. Despite Chambers' statement about him, Lawrence seems to have been always and passionately concerned with affirming man's dignity, with articulating what he considered the basic and particular dignity of twentieth-century man, whom Lawrence—somewhat like Swift—felt to be ignoring and abusing that dignity. Again like Virginia Woolf—and again despite Chambers' assertion to the contrary—Lawrence was a brilliant technical innovator. *Women in Love* (1921), for example, is in its formal departure from the novel proper not unlike *The Waves* (and far more impressive) as an attempt to formalize content at whatever cost to traditional form; and *Lady Chatterley's Lover* (1928) is, like Virginia Woolf's last novels, at once a successful expression of his perspective and a true novel in form. Unlike Huxley's—but still like Virginia Woolf's— Lawrence's thought, although "spiritual," is not orthdox.

To a certain extent the titles of their novels suggest the basic method used by the Georgians. Such titles as *The Waves, The Plumed Serpent,* and *Antic Hay* are markedly different from what are supposedly "the" titles in the English novel—*Clarissa, Tom Jones, David Copperfield, The History of Pendennis, The Mayor of Casterbridge.*

Analogy is the important literary method of our time. Before science had established the world of fact, analogy had been the way of knowing reality. Dante's four-leveled allegory and Donne's conceits, which compare the physical with the metaphysical, are examples of this metaphysical way to value and meaning. Preserved through the enlightenment only by occultists, analogy emerged again during the romantic revival. The occult studies of Blake, Rimbaud and Yeats made correspondence, as Baudelaire called it, the central preoccupation of the symbolist movement. Conrad, Joyce, and Virginia Woolf are among the novelists who followed poets away from the external, the literal and the discursive into imagistic and rhythmic suggestion. Lawrence is one of this great company.[60]

It is not true that Virginia Woolf "stood apart from her age," unconcerned with goings on in the years between the wars;[61] rather, she had "a passionate precision in collecting data about society,"[62] and—with Dorothy M. Richardson, Huxley, Joyce, and Lawrence—paid great attention to the immediate scene.

Great attention and serious attention. In an essay entitled "Le Roman anglais contemporain," published in 1927, T. S. Eliot took the Georgian novelists to task for what he called their lack of seriousness. The modern English novel, in his opinion, was deflected by a lesser psychology—psychoanalysis—away from serious psychology—James' moral preoccupation. The fault was with psychoanalysis and with that part of Dostoevski that coincides with Freud. Thus, he declared, Lawrence's world was neither our real nor ideal world, but a degenerate, uncivilized place, despite Lawrence's gifts: intensity was his sole criterion. Eliot considered Virginia Woolf most unlike Lawrence—civilized, not barbaric—but she also failed to show life: she was not "superficial" only because of her theory, which the reader must share. He considered her work most typical of the contemporary novel. Huxley was serious, but in a "chic" fashion, and sentimentally. David Garnett's "tales" were only façades, carrying the burden that man is merely an animal. James, Eliot said, was dramatic in the structure of his novels; Conrad was not, and neither were contemporary novelists.[63]

This opinion of Eliot's was a fairly early one, and can now be called a generally inadequate account of Georgian novelists. Lawrence and Virginia Woolf, at all events, are "serious" in the most profound sense of the word; Lawrence is a good deal more "civilized" than Eliot suggests, and Virginia Woolf a good deal less; *The Waves,* to cite one example, is perfectly "dramatic" according to James' own definition: "the soul of drama . . . is the portrayal . . . of a catastrophe determined in spite of oppositions."[64]

It is perhaps too soon to say whether or not Virginia Woolf was "the novelist of the Nineteen-Twenties," too soon, as well, to make any definite all-over value judgment of her work in relation to that of her contemporaries. It is not too soon to see, however imperfectly, that Virginia Woolf's literary development was determined by no isolated phenomena or personal vagaries, but had its essential counterpart in the work of her contemporaries as well; the Georgians were all attempting to provide their novels with values that would be artistically sound and acceptable.

Not until six years after *The Waves*—toward the end of the 'thirties—did Virginia Woolf publish her next novel, *The Years*. In 1941 her final novel, *Between the Acts,* was posthumously published. There is not only a gap in time before the appearance of these last novels, but also a further significant development in their philosophical and formal perspective that would seem to justify their being considered at once together and apart from the preceding novels.

Chapter V

THE LAST NOVELS

THE YEARS—possibly the best, and certainly one of the most interesting, of Virginia Woolf's novels—was published in 1937. It is by far the longest novel after *Night and Day,* and is divided into eleven sections, each of which is subdivided into several parts. The central characters of this novel are the members and friends of the large, upper-middle-class Pargiter family, followed from an afternoon in April, 1880, to a summer night in the "present day"; the setting is England, and for the most part London.

Although *The Years* resembles *The Waves* in certain respects, superficial and essential, it is not true that *The Years* is a repetition of that book,[1] that Virginia Woolf "persists in limiting herself to purely formal variations upon the same old dirge-like tune."[2] Actually, the "tune" here is no more a dirge than it was in any of the preceding novels; there is a formal variation precisely because *The Years* deals with materials ignored by *The Waves.* Like *The Waves, The Years* follows a number of people from youth to age; there are ten relatively short sections, followed by a long "summing up"; the formal perspective is a means of discovering and demonstrating a philosophical perspective that in turn gives meaning to the characters and circumstance. Descriptions of the weather begin each section of *The Years,* and such descriptions also begin many of the subdivisions within each section; of one of these, Wiget writes: "Die meterologischen Beschreibungen des Frühlings 1880 dehnen sich gleichzeitig über Stadt und Land aus, wobei ihre Auswirkungen auf das menschliche Gemüt, in einen lebhaften Rhythmus gebracht, lebhaft vor den Augen des Lesers entstehen, so dass zwischen Leser und Buch eine intime Verbindung hergestellt wird."[3] This seems true, although it is perhaps rather a subjective reaction; a more important function of these descriptions is to produce a union of apparent opposites within the novel itself: they serve the same function, but not to the same degree or in exactly the same manner, as do the descriptive passages of *The Waves*.

Despite these similarities, the differences between the two books are more important. In *The Years* all that Percival symbolized—all that was refracted to the reader only through the soliloquies of the readers—is directly apprehended. In a very limited sense *The Waves* had social consciousness; *The Years* is dependent for its effect upon immediate and extensive social consciousness. Moreover, it deals with characters from every English class; the point of view is more objectively omniscient than in *The Waves*—so that it tends to approximate dramatic point of view—and social behavior, instead of exclusive symbolism, prompts and explains individual response. In *The Waves* there were no direct conversation and no direct description of action; in *The Years* conversation and behavior are reported at length, and thought transcriptions are both relatively infrequent and brief.

The Years is concerned with good and evil, right and wrong; it can be called a justification, from Virginia Woolf's perspective, of the way of God to men. The death of Percival in *The Waves* was of course a symbol of evil; in *The Years,* however, there is no such abstraction: evil is presented not only dramatically but also immediately; good, therefore, is also presented actively—not simply as "the Good," but as this and that good behavior in society; *The Years* is a scenic novel, so that the reader remembers people and action rather than individual mood and attitude. By "facing the facts"—by managing to surmount the difficulties noted in Virginia Woolf's criticism of fiction—this novel achieves symbolic values much more impressive than those in *The Waves,* and much less dependent upon Bergsonism for their validity.

The music stopped. The young man who had been putting records on the gramophone had walked off. The couples broke apart and began to push their way through the door. They were going to eat perhaps; they were going to stream out into the back garden and sit on hard sooty chairs. The music which had been cutting grooves in [Peggy's] mind had ceased. There was a lull—a silence. Far away she heard the sounds of the London night; a horn hooted; a siren wailed on the river. The far-away sounds, the suggestion they brought in of other worlds, indifferent to this world, of people toiling, grinding, in the heart of darkness, in the depths of night, made her say over Eleanor's words, Happy in this world, happy with living people. But how can one be "happy," she asked herself, in a world bursting with misery? On every placard at every street corner was Death; or worse—tyranny; brutality; torture; the fall of civilization; the end of freedom. We here, she thought, are only sheltering under a leaf, which will be destroyed. And then Eleanor says the world is better, because two people out of all those millions are "happy."

This is the central problem of *The Years*. The idea itself is not a new one: although tyranny, loss of freedom, is now the greatest enemy, "Death" brings to mind the closing passage of *The Waves*, and it will be remembered that Clarissa Dalloway felt somehow justified in enjoying her roses and forgetting her husband's concern for the exploited, miserably poor "Albanians, or was it the Armenians?" The earlier novels hinted, in varying degrees, at the existence of the sordid and painful; *The Years* is able to present them directly as part of the immediate scene, and to make its own affirmation all the more convincing by doing so, looking at a wide world rather than an arbitrarily limited one. Again and again throughout the novel sordidity and sublimity are juxtaposed not theoretically but scenically, as they appear in concrete actions and milieus. "The shops were turning into houses; there were big houses and little houses; public houses and private houses. And here a church raised its filigree spire. Underneath were pipes, wires, drains." Both the world above the street and the world below are pictured in this novel, largely in terms of social classes.

The streets they were driving through were horribly poor; and not only poor ... but vicious. Here was the vice, the obscenity, the reality of London. It was lurid in the mixed evening light. ... Parnell. He's dead, Eleanor said to herself, still conscious of the two worlds; one flowing in wide sweeps overhead, the other tip-tapping circumscribed upon the pavement.

For "the night was full of roaring and cursing; of violence and unrest, also of beauty and joy." *The Years,* instead of selecting the beauty and joy for immediate presentation, offers the ugliness and sorrow of the life it depicts side by side with that beauty and joy, in order to justify and order the whole. When Kitty Lasswade goes to hear *Siegfried,* "the music excited her. It was magnificent. Siegfried took the broken pieces of the sword and blew on the fire and hammered, hammered, hammered. ... until at last up he swung the sword high above his head and brought it down—crack! The anvil burst asunder." This refers at once back to Kitty's tea with the Robsons—too poor for her to feel at ease with them, and whose attractive son was hammering, hammering at work when she arrived—and also forward to the sordid flat in which Maggie and Sara Pargiter are spending the same evening. Siegfried's singing has been sublime; but

"Sing something," said Maggie suddenly. Sara turned and struck the notes.
"Brandishing, flourishing my sword in my hand ..." she sang. The words were the words of some pompous eighteenth century march, but her voice was reedy and thin. Her voice broke. She stopped singing.
She sat silent with her hands on the notes. "What's the good of singing if one hasn't any voice?" she murmured.

And later

Somebody was hammering on the door of the next house ... hammer, hammer, hammer. ...
"Upcher's come home drunk and wants to be let in," said Maggie. ...
A woman's voice was heard shrieking abuse at the man. He bawled

back in a thick drunken voice from the doorstep. Then the door slammed.

They listened.

"Now he'll stagger against the wall and be sick," said Maggie.

In this way, scene is joined with scene, character juxtaposed with character, until the entire novel is an arrangement of vivid contrasts.

Behind these several contrasts is the gradual decay of Victorian culture, the gradual shift from nineteenth-century "security" to contemporary "confusion," so that those characters who are most aware wonder whether there can be any valid standard, any rule for conduct, in the midst of this continual flux. This social shift finally expresses itself in the contrast between the scene in the Pargiter home at the beginning of the novel and Delia's party at the conclusion—between the Victorian family tea and the sprawling, untidy, crowded group who sit on the floor and drink their soup from mugs; and the change is so depicted that the contrast is finally one between a static, hypocritical society and a dynamic, honest, and energetic if chaotic society.

In this change and flux two things remain constant. The weather is common to good and bad behavior, to beautiful and ugly conduct. As has been said, each section of the novel begins with a description of the weather; and in the scenes following, in which good and evil are violently juxtaposed and mingled, the weather is the same. "Over Park Lane and Piccadilly the clouds kept their freedom . . . staining windows gold, daubing them black. . . ." However—and this paradox has been noted in Virginia Woolf's earlier novels—though the weather is consistent, the weather is always changing: though beneath diversity there is unity, that unity is diversity itself. Thus the weather is a perfect symbol for Virginia Woolf's concept of unity. In exactly the same way the characters of the novel remain constant. However much they may change, age, weaken, they are always the same and always different. The problem of identity, treated in *The Waves,* reappears here, and is given a solution: North thinks:

Why not down barriers and simplify? But a world, he thought, that was all one jelly, one mass, would be a rice pudding world, a white counterpane world. To keep the emblems and tokens of North Pargiter—the man Maggie laughs at; the Frenchman holding his hat; but at the same time spread out, make a new ripple in human consciousness, be the bubble and the stream, the stream and the bubble—myself and the world together.... Anonymously.... But what do I mean, he wondered—I, to whom ceremonies are suspect and religion's dead; who don't fit ... anywhere?

The conclusion of the novel is to answer North's question.

In a review of *The Years* entitled "The End of the English Novel?" J. H. Roberts, praising the book and noting that it had "the utmost technical brilliance," nevertheless felt that Virginia Woolf was ending the life of the novel by saying that no one can know anyone else. The novel, Roberts explained, should teach its readers about other people and illumine life, but he believed Virginia Woolf's theme to be that "we live a riddle ... we shall never solve the mystery." W. H. Mellers, quoting from the novel itself, calls its theme "the passage of time and its tragedy."[5] Neither of these critics is correct.

We all think the same things; only we do not say them. It's no go, North thought. He can't say what he wants to say; he's afraid. They're all afraid; afraid of being laughed at; afraid of giving themselves away.... We're all afraid of each other, he thought; afraid of what? Of criticism; of laughter; or people who think differently.... That's what separates us; fear, he thought.

This is one of the major ideas of the novel: that people *can* know one another, but refuse to do so.

"I do not want to go back into my past, [Eleanor] was thinking. I want the present." This is another major idea: that the passage of time is anything but a tragedy; that human nature is in the process of becoming less imperfect, becoming in a creative evolution during which evil will be overcome and good triumph. This is the affirmation of the novel as a whole. Peggy mistakenly thinks that the past "was so interesting; so safe; so unreal—that past of the 'eighties; and to her, so beautiful in its unreality." But Eleanor, who has lived in that past, come through its goods and its bads, realizes that not the past but the future is safe and interesting, and that she must therefore live in the present. At the conclusion of the novel, during which Eleanor—somewhat like Bernard—has been moving toward a complete awareness, she has a final apprehension of meaning. Delia's party is breaking up; it is very late, almost dawn. Eleanor has been worrying about people's seeming inability to communicate: "She held her hands hollowed; she felt that she wanted to enclose the present moment; to make it stay; to fill it fuller and fuller, with the past the present and the future, until it shone, whole, bright, deep with understanding." At first she thinks this impossible.

It's useless, she thought, opening her hands. It must drop. It must fall. And then? she thought. For her too there would be the endless night; the endless dark. She looked ahead of her as though she saw opening in front of her a very long dark tunnel. But, thinking of the dark, something baffled her; in fact it was growing light. The blinds were white.

Here, so far, is a situation exactly like that at the conclusion of *The Waves*. But *The Years* is not content to end here, with only an abstract statement; it goes on. The caretaker's two little children enter (Delia wishes to give them cake) and sing a song: "Etho passo tanno hai, / Fai donk to tu do," and so on. No one can understand a word of what they are singing: "It was so shrill, so discordant, so meaningless." But Eleanor, looking for a word that will describe this song—this strange, new language of the youngest generation—decides upon "beautiful." Then in the dawn Eleanor goes to the window. A cab stops in front of a house two doors down.

She was watching the cab. A young man had got out; he paid the driver. Then a girl in a tweed travelling suit followed him. He fitted his latch-key to the door. "There," Eleanor murmured, as he opened the door and they stood for a moment on the threshold. "There!" she repeated as the door shut with a little thud behind them.

Then she turned round into the room. "And now?" she said ... "And now?" she asked, holding out her hands to [Morris].

With an empathy like Clarissa's—an empathy that enabled her to "become" Martin in India—Eleanor looks at the newly married couple and grasps all the immense significance of their beginning: the pattern of a continual becoming toward right and good. She has been correct in her belief that "there must be another life.... Not in dreams; but here and now, in this room, with living people.... This is too short, too broken. We know nothing, even about ourselves. We're only just beginning ... to understand, here and there." *The Years* concludes, just as *The Waves* had done, with a separate final descriptive sentence: "The sun had risen, and the sky above the houses wore an air of extraordinary beauty, simplicity and peace." This formalization of the philosophical perspective by means of immediate social and individual circumstance makes *The Years* the most persuasive of Virginia Woolf's novels. The final cab episode is additionally effective because it contrasts with a similar scene at the beginning of the novel when Delia, who wants very much to marry, watches from the same window a hansom approach the Pargiter house. And she wonders:

Was it going to stop at their door or not? ... to her regret, the cabman jerked his reins ... the cab stopped two doors lower down....

they watched a young man ... get out of the cab. He stretched up his hand to pay the driver....

The young man ran up the steps into the house; the door shut upon him and the cab drove away....

Dropping the blind, Delia turned, and coming back into the drawing-room, said suddenly:

"Oh, my God!"

Here is the idea of fulfillment and nonfulfillment; it appears very much as it had done in *The Waves*. Thus Eleanor, though she is a spinster, is fulfilled in her mental androgyny and empathy; on the other hand, Nicholas Pomjalovsky longs for a new world, and is constantly trying to make a speech in which he can articulate what he believes to be real. His inability to communicate, to surrender his identity, is symbolized—as was Neville's in *The Waves*—by his perversion. Sara Pargiter, perhaps the most pathetic person in the novel, is another example of nonfulfillment, although she herself is not entirely to blame for her inability to communicate. Extremely perceptive and sensitive, Sara is physically deformed; her behavior becomes more and more erratic as she grows older, her fantastic manner being a shield between herself and the society that she feels hostile to her. She is reduced to poverty after her parents' sudden death, and lives with her sister Maggie in a shabby walk-up flat. Maggie—who resembles Susan of *The Waves*, though she is far more human and successful a character—marries, and Sara is left alone. For a time she turns to the Church of England; she finally falls in love, but with Nicholas, who, although he loves her very much, is quite candid in explaining why he cannot marry her. Sara's final rejection of society and social intercourse is symbolized by her arriving at Delia's party—after a dinner with North in her sordid boarding house, in what is perhaps the most superbly achieved sequence in the novel—wearing one blue stocking and one white.

Although society is the immediate background of individual behavior in this novel, the use of society is not exactly conventional; it is not one social code, a single set of manners, that is emphasized, but rather the change from society to society—the social shift. As Virginia Woolf wrote in *The Waves,* "Bodies, I note, already begin to look ordinary; but what is behind them differs—the perspective." The very climax of the novel is Eleanor's dismissal of the faithful (and wonderful) Pargiter servant Crosby; together with Eleanor's sale of the Pargiter house, this constitutes her disposal of the last remnants of the old culture and tradition. This scene is filled with sadness and nostalgia; yet, although Eleanor weeps, "she was so glad." After this it is Crosby who preserves the old way, setting up pictures of the family in the little room where she boards, until "it was quite like home." For Eleanor it is not the seeming security of a traditional social context, but the apparently amorphous becoming of the future, that has value. Static society, then—as distinct from responsible human behavior—is repudiated in *The Years* too as a superimposition. This is also made clear at Delia's final party, in a "matter-spirit" contrast between Eleanor and her sister Milly. North looks at Milly and her husband Hugh—both of whom exist entirely as social creatures—and thinks, "Tut-tut-tut, and chew-chew-chew—as they trod out the soft steamy straw in the stable; as they wallowed in the primeval swamp, prolific, profuse, half-conscious." The damning word is of course "half-conscious": Milly and Hugh have regressed until in them, as in prehistoric life, awareness is choked with matter. For Eleanor—and it is toward Eleanor's point of view that North is gradually moving—life has not this static nature; it is "a perpetual discovery." She perceives life intuitionally, and "intuition may be described as turning past and present into fact directly known by transforming it from mere matter into a creative process of duration."[6] The society, like the purely social being, is residual, "half-conscious." Eleanor, with an "unreasonable exaltation," feels in her seventies "that they were all young, with the future before them. Nothing was fixed; nothing was known; life was open and free before them." How completely this agrees with Bergson may be seen in his own statement: "Consciousness corresponds exactly to the living being's power of choice; it is coextensive with ... possible action: consciousness is synonymous with invention and with freedom."[7] For just as matter is fixed, time—movement in becoming—is free. Eleanor fleetingly realizes this earlier in the novel; she leaves Maggie's home after an air raid, and looks up at the sky. "A broad fan of light, like the sail of a windmill, was sweeping slowly across the sky. It seemed to take what she was feeling and to express it broadly and simply, as if another voice were speaking in another language." This is significant, not only insofar as it underlines the function of the descriptive passages of the novel, but also when the unintelligible song of the children later recalls and emphasizes its meaning, shortly before Eleanor's own becoming brings her to complete awareness and the novel to an end. To think that the conclusion of *The Years* is "almost shocking in its irrelevance,"[8] or that the novel is "repetitious" and could have come to a close with the 1917 section just as well as with the 1937,[9] is probably to ignore or forget its meaning.

The Years has often been compared with other "period" novels of about the same time—*The Rainbow, The Old Wives' Tale,* and especially *The Forsyte Saga.* Of course *The Years* is much different from these novels,[10] and vastly superior to the last two of them. Galsworthy, however, is a few times interestingly akin to Virginia Woolf: although *The Forsyte Saga* presents human beings only as social specimens, whereas *The Years* traces Eleanor and the other Pargiters as developing individuals and as members of differing classes of a changing and developing society, nevertheless Galsworthy also toys with Bergsonistic concepts; in the "Indian Summer of a Forsyte," for example, Old Jolyon thinks of a "Life-Force."[11] But the differences between his reaction to Bergsonism and Virginia Woolf's (or Joyce's or Lawrence's) are obvious; his is a blind and fateful force, making free will impossible and people therefore irresponsible. Galsworthy's life force is antithetical to Virginia Woolf's; perhaps halfway between the two is Bernard Shaw's version, as it can be seen in such plays as *Man and Superman,* or *Heartbreak House,* or *Back to Methuselah.* For Shaw, "to be in hell is to drift: to be in heaven is to steer."[12]

Both in philosophical perspective and in social consciousness, however, *The Years* is most significantly comparable to Proust's novel. Perhaps more than any other of Virginia Woolf's novels, *The Years* both resembles and differs from *À la Recherche du temps perdu*. Both novels begin with the security of a traditional family culture, move through the First World War, and conclude with a long party scene, having traced the development of many individual characters and the transition of a society. The final section of *The Years,* indeed, is especially similar to the great party in *Le Temps retrouvé,* not only in its general proportion and significance, but in several individual details. The hypocritical upstart Mme Verdurin has finally realized her greatest dream—she, of the noble forehead and hypersensitive emotions, is Princesse de Guermantes. The framework of Proust's party, then, is very like that of Virginia Woolf's, although it is not Delia's character but her house that achieves the effect. Again there are the same painful contrasts between youth grown old and new, unknown youth; since North has been in Africa and just returned to London, the impact of the change affects him just as it affects Marcel, returned to society after his long illness. And of course there are the perceptions of reality, Marcel's before the party and Eleanor's after the party.

In *The Years,* however, no such "résurrection de la mémoire" exists as can be found in *Le Temps retrouvé* and in Virginia Woolf's own earlier novels. The whole past is not explicitly charged into the present moment as it was, for example, in *Orlando.* Eleanor, watching the newly married couple, does recapture and hold time past in time present, but this is accomplished implicitly and not given the emphasis or role it had received in the earlier books. To be sure, the present moment does shine "whole, bright, deep with understanding," and is filled "with the past the present and the future"; but it is the future—and not the past—that Eleanor realizes most emphatically. Furthermore, although she knows now that she will not disappear into "the endless night; the endless dark," it is not the sense of her own immortality that most impresses and satisfies her, but rather the sense that life is improvable as well as ever-lasting, that good can triumph over and annihilate evil. *The Years* is not a triumph of consciousness over the past so much as it is a consciousness of triumph in the future. *To the Lighthouse* concludes when Lily Briscoe, exhausted but triumphant, says, "I have had my vision" and puts aside her paintbrush. *The Years,* on the other hand, concludes with Eleanor reaching out, asking, " 'And now?' " The present moment is no longer simply an end in itself; it is at once an end and a means. *The Years* therefore overcomes what is a fairly serious limitation in Virginia Woolf's earlier novels.

This new emphasis follows quite logically from the stuff of which *The Years* is made. Eleanor as one individual realizes the present moment—perceives completely the nature of reality—as an end in itself: she has grasped the total meaning of her own life. But Eleanor as a member of society, the public as distinct from the private Eleanor, must perceive her knowledge as means rather than end. To do otherwise would be, in this case, to revert as social being to the dead Victorian culture; society cannot be conceived of as recapturing its past history, but only as using awareness of the past as a standard for future progress. The private Eleanor can say that she has had her vision; the public Eleanor, recognizing that vision as a means, must ask, " 'And now?' " As one human being, Eleanor responds; as a member of society, she must *behave* in the light of her response. "Society" and "behavior" are, in this sense, far more profound than the behavior of Milly and Hugh in the society of Delia's party. In that society, indeed, faced with that behavior, Eleanor loses her consciousness: while Milly prattles, Eleanor falls asleep:

Eleanor snored. She was nodding off, shamelessly, helplessly. There was an obscenity in unconsciousness, [North] thought. Her mouth was open; her head was on one side.

But now it was his turn. Silence gaped. One has to egg it on, he thought; somebody has to say something, or human society would cease. Hugh would cease; Milly would cease.

If this society is matter, and Eleanor's consciousness spirit, then her final awareness is Eleanor's individual victory over precisely this materiality, and her perception of a future victory for consciousness itself. Here Eleanor is defending herself from matter by falling asleep; when she wakens, she remembers her sleep as "a gap—a gap filled with the golden light of lolling candles"; this is of course the old image for spirit, the flame-candle dichotomy of "Kew Gardens." Society—real society—is not the static code of manners, but the becoming reflected in the very transition from one code to another. Value is becoming; becoming is value.

Virginia Woolf was again to employ this new emphasis upon the collective future rather than the individual past in *Between the Acts. The Years,* because of this concept of a becoming society as well as becoming individual beings, has a scope and range not to be found in any of the earlier novels; and it makes an affirmation about human life and experience more persuasive than that made by *The Waves,* where the collective becoming of Bernard's final challenge was expressed upon a purely symbolic level. Here the entire perspective has been explored, the entire significance discovered: the variegated spectacle focused by the glass roof is colored with sharp sunlight; the glass roof itself is both spectacle and sun.

Many critics have considered *The Years* a complete failure;[13] E. M. Forster was expressing a popular attitude toward this novel when he said that it was, like *Night and Day,* an "experiment in the realistic tradition. . . . as in *Night and Day,* she deserts poetry, and again she fails."[14] On the contrary, *The Years* seems to me to be Virginia Woolf's best novel; it follows consistently the essential pattern of thought seen in her earlier novels, but extends both philosophical and formal perspective further than any of them; it flawlessly formalizes a more comprehensive idea of "life itself," and it does this not by deserting what Forster calls "poetry," but by transforming and assimilating public with private values into a harmonious whole, in accordance with Virginia Woolf's vision of experience, yet justifiable outside the boundaries of that vision as it appeared in the earlier books. If by "poetry" Forster means prose style rather than exclusive symbolism, again *The Years* is considerably superior to *The Waves,* in which the "elevated style" so often becomes overemotional and gets in its own way, especially when the reader remembers that it was written by so fine a stylist as Virginia Woolf. Read hastily, *The Years* might seem no more than a "conventional novel," beautifully written—although much of it would certainly be puzzling—whereas, read carefully, it shows itself a work in which Virginia Woolf used all her treasure of technical ability to make of conventional novel form something at once traditional and new.

Virginia Woolf's last novel, *Between the Acts,* was published posthumously in 1941. It is the shortest of all her novels, and like *Mrs. Dalloway* is printed as an undivided unit except for occasional double spacings between paragraphs.* The scene is a "remote village in the very heart of England"; the action begins on a night in June, 1939, and ends on the following night, after the performance of a village pageant at Pointz Hall. The pageant itself, depicting the history of England, occupies a little more than one-sixth of the novel; it consists of a prologue suggesting the infancy of England, three acts—the Elizabethan, Augustan, and Victorian ages—and an epilogue suggesting contemporary England. The main characters of the novel are Miss La Trobe, author of the pageant, and certain members of her audience: Bartholomew Oliver, master of Pointz Hall; Lucy Swithin, his sister; Giles and Isabella Oliver, his son and daughter-in-law; Mrs. Manresa and William Dodge, Londoners who crash Pointz Hall for luncheon and remain to see the pageant. The extremely oversimplified statement of the pageant is integrated with the

* The discussion of *Between the Acts* appeared orginally, in somewhat different form, in the Summer, 1953, issue of *Accent.*

extremely complex relations between these characters to produce the novel as a whole.

The title of this novel has been explained in many ways; it indicates, in the number of meanings that can be legitimately drawn from it, the extent of symbolical suggestion through the entire novel. Joan Bennett, for example, finds "between the acts" to mean the human comedy presented between the acts of the pageant, the interval between the two World Wars, and the interval between the love of Giles and Isabella;[15] John Graham writes that "the novel as a whole is a pageant occurring literally *between the acts* of the drama which the reader himself plays before and after reading it."[16] Although each of these four meanings is justifiable and valuable, none of them seems of central importance to the novel itself. *Between the Acts,* although it embodies many of Virginia Woolf's concepts, is first and foremost a novel about free will; perhaps the title becomes clearest when "acts" is understood in the sense of "actions." Between the actions of Giles and Isabella Oliver this novel demonstrates artistically that behavior is a result not of necessity but of free will. The novel begins when, after a series of actions, Giles and Isa have paused; it concludes just before they are to begin another action: "Then the curtain rose. They spoke." The novel is not concerned with the acts themselves, but rather with what happened between the acts—specifically, with what *caused* the acts.

Freedom, in Bergsonian terms, is the condensation of clock time to mind time—of "actual time" to "mind time" in the language of *Between the Acts*—by means of perception and memory; each moment then becomes an original creation, each act a free act. Space is determinable, time is not; therefore an act motivated by and in pure-time perception is undetermined or free. "Consciousness, which is a *need of creation,* is made manifest to itself only where creation is possible. It lies dormant when life is condemned to automatism; it wakes as soon as the possibility of a choice is restored."[17] And, as has already been mentioned, "consciousness is synonymous with invention and with freedom." To be unconscious or "half-conscious" is to be enslaved. Free will exists only in pure time, but pure time is the only reality; therefore necessity is only apparent, and free will is real. Simply, then, in relation to Bergson's basic concept, life making itself (the vital impetus, spirit) is free, but life unmaking itself (matter) is doomed to necessity.[18] The will attains freedom when it ceases to be individual and becomes one with the vital impetus. So long as a person shields his identity, he cannot act with free will; when he transcends personality he achieves freedom and movement in becoming. Consciousness is freedom. Finally,

Matter [space, logical complexity] ... has no duration and so cannot last through any period of time or change: it simply *is* in the present, it does not endure but is perpetually destroyed and recreated. . . . Just as matter is absolute logical complexity memory is absolute creative synthesis. Together they constitute the hybrid notion of creative duration whose "parts" interpenetrate which, according to Bergson, comes nearest to giving a satisfactory description of the actual fact directly known which is, for him, the whole reality.[19]

These are the generalized assumptions worked into art in this novel; in them can be seen as well generalizations illustrated by various of the earlier novels. Virginia Woolf had shown, without emphasizing free will, the evolution of certain persons toward the real and their attainment of it. Clarissa Dalloway, Lily Briscoe, Orlando, Bernard, Eleanor Pargiter—all move to an awareness that they finally attain. In *Between the Acts,* however, since the emphasis differs, so also do the nature and extent of individual perception. Lucy Swithin, like Mrs. Ramsay, is shown not becoming aware but having become aware; Giles and Isa, on the other hand, though they are shown becoming aware, do not reach awareness during the course of the novel.

Mrs. Swithin is "free"; Isa is "entangled" and, with Giles and

William Dodge, "caught and caged." Mrs. Swithin, more than seventy years old, "was given to increasing the bounds of the moment by flights into past or future"; she walks "as if the floor were fluid"; her favorite book is an outline of history, and her comments and thoughts about this book not only symbolize her own pure-time existence but also give the novel itself an almost infinite scope. She is nicknamed "Old Flimsy"; and "flimsy" is in newspaper jargon a semitransparent paper. Mrs. Swithin, then, is spirit. "Above, the air rushed; beneath was water. She stood between two fluidities...."

In direct contrast to Lucy is her brother Bart. "For she belonged to the unifiers; he to the separatists." She represents faith, and he reason. Bart, impatient with Lucy's tendency to exaggerate, in love with facts and distrustful of her impressions, resembles Mr. Ramsay of *To the Lighthouse:* here, too, there is talk about the weather:

"It's very unsettled. It'll rain, I'm afraid. We can only pray," she added, and fingered her crucifix.
"And provide umbrellas," said her brother.

Mrs. Swithin's crucifix, worn on a chain about her neck, is important: *Between the Acts* is the only one of Virginia Woolf's novels in which a sympathetic character is Christian, and in which Christianity itself is treated with anything like sympathy. Mrs. Swithin is an extremely devout woman; to be sure, religion is mainly a symbol for the spiritual life, as Bart's thought about it indicates:

It was not in books the answer to his question—why, in Lucy's skull, shaped so much like his own, there existed a prayable being? She didn't, he supposed, invest it with hair, teeth or toenails. It was, he supposed, more of a force or a radiance, controlling the thrush and the worm; the tulip and the hound; and himself, too, an old man with swollen veins. It got her out of bed on a cold morning and sent her down the muddy path to worship it, whose mouthpiece was Streatfield.

Although bumbling Streatfield is no hero, religion in this novel has more than symbolic value. The purpose of the pageant is to raise money for the installation of electric lights in the village church— the modernization, the "illumination" of the church. Further, although the old chapel at Pointz Hall is now used as a larder, nevertheless the question is asked:

Can the Christian faith adapt itself? In times like these ... At Larting no one goes to church ... There's the dogs, there's the pictures. ... It's odd that science, so they tell me, is making things (so to speak) more spiritual ... The very latest notion, so I'm told is, nothing's solid ... There, you can get a glimpse of the church through the trees.

And William Dodge, who looks at Mrs. Swithin's crucifix and wonders: "How could she weight herself down by that sleek symbol? How stamp herself, so volatile, so vagrant, with that image?" is himself physically "undecided as to sex"[20] and unable to communicate because of his attachment to his own identity.

The pageant, if it has the purpose of illuminating the church, has also the purpose of illuminating the novel. In a series of excellent parodies of English drama, written mostly in very bad verse, Miss La Trobe has tried to set forth her vision. Although the city council has neglected to bring water to the village, Miss La Trobe has written her pageant: although, that is doubtless to say, government cannot give order or meaning to human life, art—even it would seem bad art—can. The pageant, by placing the English past into the present day, accomplishes for the audience on one level what Mrs. Swithin has been able to accomplish for herself on another. Naturally Mrs. Swithin appreciates what Miss La Trobe has done, and thanks her:

"Oh Miss La Trobe!" [Lucy] exclaimed; and stopped. Then she began again; "Oh Miss La Trobe, I do congratulate you! ... What a small part I've had to play! but you've made me feel I could have played ... Cleopatra!" ...

"I might have been—Cleopatra," Miss La Trobe repeated. "You've stirred in me my unacted part," she meant.

The pageant is acted by villagers, so that it becomes a dramatization of consciousness. Just as the actors, annihilating their own identities in the English past, attain freedom, so the present moment, itself inseparable from the past, becomes free; so also Isa and Giles at the conclusion of the novel begin a free act, after the irresoluteness that has characterized them during the day. They are left alone:

Giles crumpled the newspaper and turned out the light. Left alone together for the first time that day, they were silent. Alone, enmity was bared; also love. Before they slept, they must fight; after they had fought, they would embrace. From that embrace another life might be born. But first they must fight, as the dog fox fights with the vixen, in the heart of darkness, in the fields of night.

Isa let her sewing drop. The great hooded chairs had become enormous. And Giles, too. And Isa too against the window. The window was all sky without colour. The house had lost its shelter. It was night before roads were made, or houses. It was the night that dwellers in caves had watched from some high place among rocks.

Then the curtain rose. They spoke.

Here the Bergsonian prerequisites for free will have been attained: the whole past is in the present, so that the present moment is no longer spatialized; the past is a purely temporal past, so that the present moment will be a creation, a unique achievement—this act will be the first act ever to have been done; Isa and Giles have shed their immediate identity and become "enormous." They are the actors, acting the play; there is no longer a difference between the pageant world and the actual world, for past and present have become one in pure time.

It is art that has made this act possible. The pageant has supplied for Giles and Isa the consciousness that they themselves could not achieve and no doubt do not recognize. Isa has been distracted by an attraction for Rupert Haines; Giles has been upset over the state of world affairs and an attraction for Mrs.

Manresa, that "wild child of nature." Their lust, like the lust of William Dodge for Giles, has caused them to separate present from past. Giles, indeed, repeating the line "Where there's a Will there's a Way," from the pageant, sees in that only a prompting to pursue Mrs. Manresa. He refuses consciousness; walking to the barn he notices that

couched in the grass, curled in an olive green ring, was a snake. Dead? No, choked with a toad in its mouth. The snake was unable to swallow; the toad was unable to die. A spasm made the ribs contract; blood oozed. It was birth the wrong way round—a monstrous inversion. So, raising his foot, he stamped on them. The mass crushed and slithered. The white canvas on his tennis shoes was bloodstained and sticky. But it was action. Action relieved him.

This is symbolic of action that interpenetrates the conscious states, disrupting consciousness, interrupting the creative evolution of the memory that precedes the free act. This too is "birth the wrong way round—a monstrous inversion," for it moves away from awareness and creative perception to material action, in a path opposite to that of the vital impetus. The play, however, supplies for Giles and Isa the consciousness they lack, and enables them to act freely and creatively. It is perhaps in this sense that the pageant will provide "illumination." Since the pageant is a representation of consciousness, a denial of spatialized identity, it can encourage the awareness of Giles and Isa in their becoming even though it does not accomplish that awareness. Thus as the spectators move away after the pageant, several of them illustrate by their remarks about it the kind of effect it can have. Although some dismiss it as "utter bosh," and some accept meekly the halfway interpretation of Streatfield, a few manage to work with the play: "Or was that, perhaps, what [Miss La Trobe] meant? ... that if we don't jump to conclusions, if you think, and I think, perhaps one day, thinking differently, we shall think the same?"[21] Their very search for meaning is in a sense the meaning itself, as part of their becoming.

Giles and Isa, like Eleanor in *The Years,* have public as well as private significance when, at the conclusion of *Between the Acts,* they begin to act, to use as well as receive their growing awareness. As Warren Beck has pointed out in his rewarding study of this novel, it is more than a coincidence that Isa's age—thirty-nine—is also the age of the century: *Between the Acts* "relate[s] the flow of individual consciousness to large political and social contours of the past and present."[22] It is for social as well as individual reasons, with public as well as private implications, that these characters are "caught," "entangled"; just as Lucy Swithin's outline of history combines with the pageant to give this novel temporal breadth, so also Giles' preoccupation with the disastrous state of affairs in Europe gives it spatial breadth and lends social significance to the characters' attitudes and behavior. Another war might well be, like the First World War in *Jacob's Room,* the surrender of consciousness to destructive and unthoughtful action.

In *The Years* it was Delia's party that depicted the chaotic—and mobile—state of contemporary life. In *Between the Acts* it is the epilogue of the pageant that serves this purpose. The third act has been concerned with the static and sterile Victorian age, in which a policeman stands, *"truncheon in hand, guarding respectability, and prosperity, and the purity of Victoria's land,"* and singing "'Ome, Sweet 'Ome." Then comes an interval, during which members of the audience argue about the worth of Victorian values. After a symbolic transition—rain falls, a tableau shows the rebuilding of civilization after the war—the gramophone plays a waltz; birds fly about in time to the music; "perched on the wall, they seemed to foretell what after all the *Times* was saying yesterday. Homes will be built. Each flat with its refrigerator, in the crannied wall. Each of us a free man; plates washed by machinery; not an aeroplane to vex us; all liberated; made whole." How well this prophecy has been fulfilled is suggested throughout the pageant by the behavior of the gramophone: referred to as "the machine," it is constantly breaking down, and "chuff, chuff, chuff" or "tick, tick, tick" takes the place of music. The machine is also clock time:

Time went on and on like the hands of the kitchen clock. (The machine chuffed in the bushes.) If [the Victorians] had met with no resistance . . . nothing wrong, they'd still be going round and round and round. . . . Change had to come . . . or there'd have been yards and yards of Papa's beard, of Mama's knitting. . . . change had to come, unless things were perfect; in which case . . . they resisted Time.

Mrs. Swithin is perfect: " 'I don't believe,' " she says, " 'that there ever were such people. Only you and me and William dressed differently.' "

The machine now proceeds to play cacophonic rhythms instead of the smooth measures of the waltz; the actors suddenly appear before the audience carrying mirrors, "and the audience saw themselves, not whole by any means, but at any rate sitting still." With the exception of Mrs. Manresa, who takes advantage of her mirror by powdering her nose, the spectators refuse to look at themselves. As they sit embarrassedly evading their reflections, a voice from the megaphone offers them the "moral" of the pageant: they are, indeed, despicable and base, yet they have certain redeeming qualities—*"the resolute refusal of some pimpled dirty little scrub in sandals to sell his soul,"* for example. If the mirrors reflect them as "scraps, orts and fragments," yet the music from the gramophone—a familiar melody begins— affirms that they are whole and united.

Like quicksilver sliding, filings magnetized, the distracted united. The tune began; the first note meant a second; the second a third. Then down beneath a force was born in opposition; then another. On different levels they diverged. On different levels ourselves went forward; flower gathering some on the surface; others descending to wrestle with the meaning; but all comprehending; all enlisted. The whole population of the mind's immeasurable profundity came flocking; from the unprotected, the unskinned; and dawn rose; and azure; from chaos and cacophony measure; but not the melody of surface sound alone controlled it; but also the warring battle-plumed warriors straining asunder: To part? No. Compelled from the ends of the horizon; recalled from the edge of appalling crevasses; they crashed; solved; united.

There follows an interpretation of the pageant by the Reverend Streatfield—"an intolerable constriction, contraction, and reduction to simplified absurdity he was to be sure!" The pageant, he feels, has said that " 'we are members one of another. Each is part of the whole. . . . Dare we, I asked myself, limit life to ourselves? May we not hold that there is a spirit that inspires, pervades. . . .' " This is of course intended as a Christian interpretation—"Scraps, orts and fragments! Surely, we should unite?" But he is interrupted by the sound of a formation of airplanes flying overhead: the apparent unity is disrupted.

As she had done in previous novels, Virginia Woolf here again rejects traditional mysticism, with its belief in one beneath the many. Despite its superficial resemblance to her own perspective, Streatfield's is really much different. In *Between the Acts* as in the earlier novels, it is not the one that Virginia Woolf affirms; denying the one, denying the many, she affirms the manyness beneath the many; the airplanes' interruption, which destroys Streatfield's interpretation, at the same time illustrates Virginia Woolf's by its suggestion of a changeless change, an unceasing mobility, in comparison with which traditional mysticism is static. "The gramophone was affirming in tones there was no denying, triumphant yet valedictory: *Dispersed are we; who have come together. But,* the gramophone asserted, *let us retain whatever made that harmony. . . .* The gramophone gurgled *Unity—Dispersity.* It gurgled *Un . . . dis . . .* And ceased." It is precisely the interruption that is the unity.

This paradox appears as well in the title and central problem of the novel. It is between the acts that the acts are really accomplished; to will freely is precisely to remain indeterminate, mobile, in consciousness of pure time existence: the self "lives and develops by means of its very hesitations, until the free action drops from it like an overripe fruit."²³ The only true stability is change, for immobility is death. Isa, who secretly writes poetry (and grim poetry it must be), thinks in what can be called verse throughout the novel; and there is a correspondence between the imagery and themes of her poetry and the movement of the book itself. Her poetry reflects an awareness of which Isa is not immediately conscious; between the acts of the pageant she "turned in the direction of the stable"—"stable" in both concrete and abstract senses—and thinks: "Where do I wander?... Down what draughty tunnels? Where the eyeless wind blows? And there grows nothing for the eye. No rose. To issue where? In some harvestless dim field where no evening lets fall her mantle; nor sun rises. All's equal there. Unblowing, ungrowing are the roses there. Change is not; nor the mutable and lovable; nor greetings and partings; nor furtive findings and feelings, where hand seeks hand and eye seeks shelter from the eye." Without change, mutability, the "rise and fall and fall and rise again," there cannot be life. It is because of change that at the conclusion of the novel "another life might be born"—another social as well as individual life, the "New World" of *The Years*.

Miss La Trobe, for her part, thinks of this stability of instability with the same imagery that Virginia Woolf had used in *Orlando;* the audience at first, she thinks, "glared as if they were exposed to a frost that nipped them and fixed them all at the same level. Only Bond the cowman looked fluid and natural." And when the wind carries away the words of the actors, so that the audience cannot understand, she thinks, "This is death"; but when the cows begin suddenly to bellow, so that "it was the primeval voice sounding loud in the ear of the present moment," Miss La Trobe exclaims, " 'Thank Heaven!' " Consciousness is mobility and life. On another level, Miss La Trobe as artist illustrates this concept: it is not in contemplation of a finished work that she finds happiness, but in preparation for a new and better work. At the end of the day she sits over a drink planning another play. "She set down her glass. She heard the first words." Neither the pageant of that afternoon nor the present moment in the village public house satisfies Miss La Trobe; instead, she lives in and for the becoming of her next play.

Her planning, her sudden hearing of the first words—so obviously a counterpart to the concluding passage of the novel—underline that comparison between the progress of art and the progress of life with which the whole book has been concerned. In both cases the emphasis, like that of *The Years,* is different from the emphasis of the earlier novels, different from the emphasis of Bergson or Proust. Lily Briscoe was content to have finished her painting, in *To the Lighthouse;* it was a bad picture; it would be hidden in some attic; nevertheless she had completed it. Lily comes to rest as soon as she has had her vision. Miss La Trobe, on the other hand, is painfully conscious of the faults in her pageant, and though it is completed she is not at rest. Rather, she is using the past as a means for the future, seeing her new play in the light of what she has already done. It is, furthermore, not in an ivory tower or paneled library, but in a public house heavy with smoke and conversation, that she works—amid the flux of life instead of seemingly escaped from it. If the novel of Virginia Woolf is a "glass roof," nevertheless her characters are with very few exceptions certainly not "people under glass."

In *The Years* it had been suggested that "we all think the same things; only we do not say them." In *Between the Acts* this idea finds formal expression, just as the idea that "nothing was simply one thing" had done in *The Waves.* Mrs. Swithin says at one point: " 'We haven't the words—we haven't the words. . . . Behind the eyes; not on the lips; that's all.' " At the pageant, therefore, although each person sees the play somewhat differently, the audience tends to think about the play collectively—there are passages in which neither the author nor any one of the charatcers is thinking the thoughts transcribed, but in which the audience as a whole is thinking identically.

The tune hummed:

> *The King is in his counting house,*
> *Counting out his money,*
> *The Queen is in her parlour*
> *Eating...*

Suddenly the tune stopped. The tune changed. A waltz, was it? Something half known, half not. The swallows danced it. Round and round, in and out they skimmed. Real swallows. Retreating and advancing. And the trees, O the trees, how gravely and sedately like senators in council, or the spaced pillars of some cathedral church.... Yes, they barred the music, and massed and hoarded; and prevented what was fluid from overflowing. The swallows—or martins were they?—The temple-haunting martins who come, have always come....

The tune changed; snapped; broke; jagged. Fox-trot was it? Jazz? Anyhow the rhythm kicked, reared, snapped short. What a jangle and a jingle! Well, with the means at her disposal, you can't ask too much. What a cackle, a cacophony! Nothing ended. So abrupt. Such an outrage; such an insult; And not plain. Very up to date, all the same. What is her game?

This begins as a statement by the author, but becomes a transcription of the thoughts of a large part of the audience. In this passage the audience has a conventional reaction to what is going on; in other passages the collective thinking, presented dramatically, is in agreement with the attitude of the central intelligence. When Streatfield rises to speak, for example, "of all incongruous sights a clergyman in the livery of his servitude to the summing up was the most grotesque and entire. He opened his mouth. O Lord, protect and preserve us from words the defilers, from words the impure! What need have we of words to remind us? Must I be Thomas, you Jane?" That prayer is neither the author's nor any one of the characters'; rather it is a transcription of collective consciousness, much as the soliloquies in *The Waves* were transcriptions of individual response. This device is used here only occasionally; had Virginia Woolf lived to write another novel, she might have used it more pervasively.

Between the Acts has brought forth from its critics remarkably contradictory and extreme opinions.[24] According to Louis Kronenberger, this novel, "by all means her weakest . . . represents only another step in her steady creative decline [and is] merely from start to finish an evasion of the problems it raises. It introduces us to people, some of them with frustrated and fractured lives, and, instead of exploring them, makes us sit with them while they watch a pageant . . . the pasteboard dramas completely overshadow the flesh-and-blood ones. Even an ironic intention of showing that the real people are as dead and done for as the stage puppets cannot justify . . . dabbling in human beings. . . . The book ends with two of the real people about to confront each other: it should, of course, have begun there."[25] Philip Rahv calls it Virginia Woolf's "most unhappy book."[26] Warren Beck and Joan Bennett, however, give it high praise,[27] and Walter Allen thinks it "among the finest novels of our time."[28] This last opinion seems gradually to be growing more and more popular. For the most part it seems that those critics who have extended readers' awareness of the complexities and meaning of *Between the Acts*—and of them Warren Beck is most notable—have tended to give it a prominent place among Virginia Woolf's books, whereas those to whom it is not an interesting novel have naturally enough dismissed it. It is perhaps significant, at any rate, that *Between the Acts* has almost always been rated either very high or very low, seldom mediocre.

Probably the most adequate valuation is James S. Wilson's: Wilson thought *Between the Acts* "a completed novel but perhaps an unfinished work of art."[29] Even if *Between the Acts* is considered as potentially more comprehensive than *The Years,* certainly it does not equal *The Years* as an achievement.

Leonard Woolf, in a note prefixed to *Between the Acts,* explains that "the MS. of this book had been completed, but had not been finally revised for the printer, at the time of Virginia Woolf's death. She would not, I believe, have made any large or material alterations in it, though she would probably have made a good many small corrections or revisions before passing the final proofs." This seems, in view of the book itself, to justify Wilson's statement. As a novel, *Between the Acts* is a finished product: its form is in every way consistent and expressive. But as a "work of art"—that is to say, in the smaller but important matters of prose style and texture, and even in so relatively unimportant a thing as punctuation—it is not quite finished in comparison with the earlier novels. Isa's poetic reveries, for example, are neither good enough as poetry to be stylistically justified in their own right nor yet always quite bad enough to stand away from context: they are not poetry, but it is difficult to be certain that they were not intended by the author as poetry. The poetry of the pageant has no such ambiguity—it is clearly the rather clumsy expression of a sincere poetess, Miss La Trobe, at the same time that it is symbolic of Miss La Trobe's general difficulties, for one reason or another, with her work. But Isa's poetry is neither good nor *significantly* bad. Perhaps, to be sure, the flaw is one that Virginia Woolf herself did not notice, but that is doubtful—despite the often overelaborate prose of *The Waves*—since her earlier works do not usually suffer from such flaws. Rather, it is probable that after her revisions this blemish would have been remedied. Her comments upon this point in the diary are ambiguous. However, *Between the Acts* must be read as it is, and not as it might or would or should have been; and, as it is, it has not the total precision of, say, *To the Lighthouse* or *The Years*.

Although *Between the Acts* is "an unfinished work of art" according to the standard set by Virginia Woolf's own previous works, it is one of her most important novels, because it manages at once to relate public and private values in its expression of her more comprehensive and appealing philosophical perspective, and to do that against a background so cosmic as to invest almost every particular in the book with universal implications. Again, because of such formal potentialities as the extreme condensation and the transcriptions of collective response, *Between the Acts* is important, not only in itself and as the last of Virginia Woolf's novels, but also as a fresh step in her continual endeavor to "prepare the way for masterpieces to come."[30]

Chapter VI

CONCLUSION

A<small>N ACCOUNT</small> of any works of art which emphasizes, as this one has tended to emphasize, abstract meaning very often runs the risk of implying that understanding of an author's philosophical perspective is the same as understanding of his entire art: that a novelist, for example, is to be thought of simply as a philosopher who writes fiction. But, although perhaps some novelists are concerned primarily with ideas per se, Virginia Woolf is clearly not one of them. It would therefore be unfair to valuate her achievement merely by valuating the comparative importance and profundity of her thought when that thought has been reëxpressed in conceptual terms. However, it is just as unfair to ignore or minimize that raw material as to make of it the sole criterion by which her novels are to be judged. Virginia Woolf has been a victim of the former method—has been labeled "impressionist" and "pessimist" and "without ideas"—to such an extent that possibly an overemphasis of conceptual meaning in her novels would be the only way of bringing them back into clear focus. At any rate, it seems impossible adequately to understand those novels as works of art without first gaining the philosophical perspective from which they were written: that much has been suggested by the very lack of agreement as to their artistic worth. And gaining the perspective simply means looking at the novels for what they are—literary experiences, in which concept has been imaginatively expressed as art, as significant form. The "point," goodness knows, is not to recover the concept for itself, but to discover the *art,* the concept in action.

To be sure, Virginia Woolf is not an easy novelist; her philosophical perspective and, because of it, her formal perspective are complex enough to exasperate some critics; and "there has been enough comment on difficulty to warn off any reader who doesn't happen to agree with St. Thomas Aquinas that beauty— even like truth and goodness—is one of the most difficult things in the world, demanding a strenuous effort, which, in the end, is more than adequately rewarded."[1] To apprehend the exact form, the exact meaning, of a novel like *The Years*—rather than to suppose it no more than formless according to conventional standards—is difficult and rewarding, for two reasons: first, be-cause Virginia Woolf was a serious novelist; second, because, in her own words, "when philosophy is not consumed in a novel, when we can underline this phrase with a pencil, and cut out that exhortation with a pair of scissors and paste the whole into a system, it is safe to say that there is something wrong with the philosophy or with the novel or with both." Furthermore, if meaning is to be expressed artistically it must be expressed, not residually as philosophy, but dynamically as form. Thus "what is done so deliberately is done with a purpose. This defiance of the ordinary, these airs and graces ... are all there to create an atmosphere that is unlike that of daily life, to prepare the way for a new and original sense of the human scene."[2]

In *The Voyage Out* the form, although complex and success-ful, is also quite conventional; the novel is a tragedy that affirms empirical values. It contains, however, the germs of concepts very different from those that determined it. In *Night and Day* the new concepts are affirmed and used without, however, being clearly defined; *Night and Day* thus becomes a novel of man-ners which denies that manners give valid expression to "life itself"—a novel in which the form is contradictory to the in-tended meaning.

Jacob's Room is an unsuccessful attempt to modify conven-tional novel form in accordance with a view of life that even the modification is insufficient to express in any sustained fash-ion, so that "Jacob himself," whom the novel is supposed to cap-ture, escapes, and only his "room" remains. But with *Mrs.*

Dalloway Virginia Woolf first gave adequate expression in novel form to her philosophical perspective, which, now that it is defined artistically, is found to be most conveniently representable as concept in Bergsonian terms. The form of this novel, like that of the short stories in *Monday or Tuesday,* is an expression of the philosophical perspective rather than a modification to suit it.

To the Lighthouse, Orlando, and *The Waves* represent successive advances in the creative modulation of philosophical and formal perspective. *To the Lighthouse* can be said to illustrate the Bergsonistic vision of life and experience that *Mrs. Dalloway* had defined; *Orlando,* introducing still more concepts, expresses them in fantasy form; *The Waves,* a complete departure from the form of the novel proper, is at the same time a successful formal expression of certain ideas—that "nothing was simply one thing," for example—found in the earlier novels.

The Years and *Between the Acts* emphasize public as well as personal values—"future becoming" as well as re-creation of time past in the present moment. Because these novels have so wide a scope, because they posit values verifiable outside the limits of Bergsonistic concept, they can be called the most comprehensive formalizations of Virginia Woolf's philosophical perspective, just as *The Waves* can be called the most intensive.

But *Between the Acts* cannot be neatly labeled as the terminus of Virginia Woolf's literary development; it contains potentialities that, to judge by the configuration of that development, would have been the starting points for still different novels if Virginia Woolf had lived. On the other hand, neither can the novels be labeled "experiments," unless it is first realized that, after *Night and Day* and *Jacob's Room,* each of them is successful in accomplishing all that it sets out to accomplish. To say that "when other novelists have made her experiments an organic part of the novel, her value will begin to decline to that of an experimental and transitional writer"[8] is perhaps to confuse successful with unsuccessful experiments—to see no difference between *Jacob's Room* and *To the Lighthouse,* or between *Night and Day* and *The Years.*

Virginia Woolf's prose style has always been given great praise and, it is fairly safe to say, will continue to be admired; at her best she is without doubt one of the great writers of English prose. Again, she is not seldom presented with such compliments as being called "the novelist most flawless in her taste of all the English."[4] And yet, as has been noted, she herself believed that "the success of the masterpieces seems to lie not so much in their freedom from faults—indeed we tolerate the grossest errors in them all—but in the immense persuasiveness of a mind which has completely mastered its perspective."[5] It is for this mastery of her perspective, for "the immense persuasiveness" of thought as art in six or seven of her novels, that Virginia Woolf deserves most notice: her style and her taste are ancillary, however important and admirable they may be; they augment, but do not constitute, her achievement as a writer of prose fiction.

If, then, six or seven of Virginia Woolf's novels can be called, by her own rigorous standard at least, "masterpieces"—if she can be called, when considered not only in the light of what she tried to do but also in the light of what she succeeded in doing, a great artist as well as an intelligent thinker—why is it a bit embarrassing to remember that Katherine Anne Porter spoke of Virginia Woolf as being "a profound genius of the first order"?[6] Why does denial of that assertion seem in a sense higher praise than agreement with it? Of Dante and Shakespeare, even of Dostoevski perhaps, that statement is probably true; of Proust or Lawrence it is probably not; it is probably not true of Virginia Woolf. Her philosophical perspective in itself was to a considerable extent responsible for Virginia Woolf's success as an artist; might it also have been responsible, to a greater extent, for her limitations? A Bergsonian metaphysic may not have the caliber of "profound genius of the first order." No matter how successfully it is used for artistic purposes, no matter how successful the artistic achievement that employs it, Bergsonism seems not to be thought essentially profound, not essentially a metaphysic of the first order. "What is this creative purpose that must wait for sun and rain to set in motion? What is this life that in any individual can be suddenly extinguished by a bullet? What is this *élan vital* that a little fall in temperature would banish altogether from the universe?"[7] So wrote Santayana, and of course he is not the only philosopher to have taken the very backbone of Bergsonism for a target. Profound at times, brilliant and perceptive in parts, imaginative itself as a work of art, Bergson's philosophy seems nevertheless weak and self-contradictory as a whole unless it is accepted with almost complete intellectual abeyance. So also is part of the abstract thought of Virginia Woolf, which closely corresponds to Bergson's except perhaps in the last two novels.

It may be correct to argue, however, that Virginia Woolf is not a philosopher but a novelist. Her world is artistically valid if it is honest and self-consistent within the novels; since it does not demand acceptance outside the novels—as Bergson's world demands acceptance outside his writings—Virginia Woolf is, so to speak, a better artist than Bergson is a philosopher. She is doubtless a great artist, despite her several limitations, some of them serious enough; but still "profound genius of the first order" is really an extraliterary valuation that most of her thought, as thought, may not justify. What can be safely said of Virginia Woolf is that "by rendering what she called reality's 'luminous halo,' [she] has reminded a tragically preoccupied generation of the dynamic mystery of mind, which becomes the one enduring source of fortitude and a common hope; and hence remains a central theme for literary art; [that] Virginia Woolf may yet be seen as one of the period's most profoundly realistic and discerning artists."[8]

What effect will the nature of her philosophical perspective have upon Virginia Woolf's reputation as novelist in the future?

Would she have been a better novelist if she had never swerved from the more general and hence more permanent perspective of *The Voyage Out?* Has she, by rejecting that perspective, really presented a valid interpretation of life—one that will continue to be significant experience for future readers? At present such questions as these can be met only with conjecture; yet they would be of vital importance for the historian of literature. And if such a texture of questions is disconcerting, it can be remembered that the same questions were asked of George Eliot and Comtism: they have been answered so as to leave George Eliot among the very greatest novelists no matter where Comtism may be.

It can also be remembered that if Virginia Woolf had not swerved from the perspective of *The Voyage Out*—if she had been unable to achieve what was for her a more satisfying philosophical perspective—she might very well have written nothing after *Night and Day;* that, on the other hand, in her last novels she formalizes a vision of experience that, although *for her* it developed out of a Bergsonistic perspective, is to a large extent independent of that perspective and can be substantiated even as concept without recourse to Bergsonism. The philosophical perspective of *The Years* enabled Virginia Woolf to form conclusions about the meaning of human life that are every bit as general, as classical, as those in *The Voyage Out,* and far more persuasively and beautifully communicated.

NOTE ON THE NAMES OF VIRGINIA WOOLF'S CHARACTERS

That Virginia Woolf did not select names for her characters in haphazard fashion can be seen even if the meanings of only her major women's names are considered:

Rachel: sheep or lamb; innocence
Helen: light; bright as the sun
Katharine: pure, virtuous
Clara: shining; brilliant
Clarissa: fair; pure; or the same as Clara
Lily: the flower, a symbol of purity
Orlando: the country's glory
Susan: a lily
Eleanor: the same as Helen
Lucy: light; born at daybreak

It is surely no coincidence that each of these names with the exception of Orlando denotes either purity or light, especially when we recall the flame-candle image for spirit and matter, and the purity of that spirit—the "luminous halo," the "semi-transparent envelope" to which Virginia Woolf likened "life itself" or consciousness. Further, Helen, Eleanor, and Lucy all refer to the dawn, which is so important a symbol in *The Waves* and *The Years*. Orlando, though an exception, is suitable insofar as that character represents on one level the sum total of English consciousness, and also because of Victoria Sackville-West's poem *The Land*—with which Orlando's "The Oak Tree" is identical—celebrating the beauty and fertility of England.

In the same way, Bernard is a "strong warrior"; Jacob and James both mean "supplanter"; Marmaduke—Orlando's sailor husband—is a "naval commander."

There are some exceptions, however, to this harmony between name and person. Of these the most startling is Doris; Miss

Kilman's name, though it can mean "gift of God," can also mean "from the sea"! Kilman is perhaps sufficient comment in this case. Again, Virginia Woolf uses William for three fairly important and unsympathetic characters—William Rodney, Sir William Bradshaw, and William Dodge—although this name, which can mean "defender," "protector of many," "shield," or "famous," does not seem to be especially appropriate, except ironically for the first two Williams.

Mrs. Ramsay is of course nameless. Ramsay, from Ram's Island (Ram being a former name meaning "stalwart"), is after all not her name but her husband's, and she is never called by a given name: simply, she is "life itself."

NOTES

NOTES TO CHAPTER I

INTRODUCTION

(Pages 1–7)

[1] *Virginia Woolf, Her Art as a Novelist*, p. 64.

[2] *Virginia Woolf—A Commentary*, pp. 54ff., 189, 210, 212.

[3] *Virginia Woolf*, p. 54.

[4] *Le Roman psychologique de Virginia Woolf*, pp. 129, 140–157.

[5] *The English Novel in Transition 1885–1940*, pp. 214–216.

[6] *Virginia Woolf*, p. 20ff.

[7] *La Philosophie de Virginia Woolf*, pp. 3–4.

[8] *Virginia Woolf*, p. 76.

[9] *The Twentieth Century Novel*, p. 493.

[10] *An Assessment of Twentieth-Century Literature*, p. 88.

[11] *Virginia Woolf—A Study*, p. 38.

[12] The best biographical account of Virginia Woolf to date is in Winifred Holtby's book, pp. 9–36.

[13] Her mother wrote a small book, *Notes from Sick Rooms* (London: Smith Elder, 1883), some passages of which, it has been noted, are in their humor suggestive of her own style. Mrs. Stephen was the model for Mrs. Ramsay in *To the Lighthouse*.

[14] These were the real "members," according to Stephen Spender (*World Within World*, pp. 126–128), who adds that E. M. Forster and T. S. Eliot were "associated" but not "belonging." Others who have been called part of the group include Desmond MacCarthy, Charles Tennyson, Hilton Young (Lord Kennett), Arthur Waley, John Maynard Keynes, Saxon Sydney Turner, G. Lowes Dickinson, Elizabeth Bowen, Rosamond Lehmann, Duncan Grant, Hugh Walpole, Lady Ottoline Morrell, Ethel Sands, Bertrand Russell, the Sitwells, Leonard Woolf, Charles Sanger, Theodore Llewelyn Davies, and Spender himself. You can, it would seem, make of the "Bloomsbury Group" what you will.

[15] Duncan Grant, "Virginia Woolf," p. 405.

[16] London: Rupert Davis, 1949, pp. 78–103. Clive Bell's writings, profoundly indebted to Moore, bear testimony to his importance for the group. Virginia Woolf's work shows no trace of Moore's influence; her theory may have been somewhat affected by R. A. M. Stevenson's *Velasquez* (London: George Bell and Sons, 1900), another book popular in "Bloomsbury," as J. Isaacs has pointed out (*An Assessment of Twentieth-Century Literature*, p. 87). In connection with the title "Bloomsbury Group," see R. F. Harrod, *The Life of John Maynard Keynes*, p. 174n.

[17] Review of *Two Memoirs*, pp. 242–246.

[18] "Virginia Woolf," *Horizon*, pp. 315–316.

[19] This date is given by Pelham Edgar, *The Art of the Novel*, p. 473. Duncan Grant, *op. cit.*, p. 405, says that the novel "took seven years to finish," however.

[20] See *Time*, April 14, 1941, pp. 34, 36; May 5, 1941, p. 97.

[21] William Plomer, "Virginia Woolf," p. 325.

[22] Daiches, *Virginia Woolf*, p. 156; *Time*, May 5, 1941, p. 97. Daiches explains that the second sentence of this note "was consistently misquoted in the press"; hence the erroneous reasons offered for the suicide, which Leonard Woolf corrected by explaining the note.

[23] "Mr. Bennett and Mrs. Brown," in *The Captain's Death Bed*, p. 91.

NOTES TO CHAPTER II

THE EARLY NOVELS

(Pages 8–39)

[1] F. C. Frierson, *The English Novel in Transition 1885–1940*, p. 305.

[2] The beginning of H. G. Wells' *Tono-Bungay* (1909).

[3] F. M. Ford, *The Good Soldier* (1915; New York: Boni, 1927, p. 158). The "character" is here a personal reference required by a servant.

[4] J. Isaacs, *Assessment*, p. 26, believes that it was this event to which Virginia Woolf referred in "Mr. Bennett and Mrs. Brown."

[5] Delattre, *Le Roman*, p. 61.

[6] Isaacs, *Assessment*, pp. 27–28.

[7] Heineman, 1912–1915.

[8] "The Russian Point of View," *Common Reader*, pp. 249ff.

[9] See Frierson, *op. cit.*, pp. 141–142.

[10] D. H. Lawrence, *The Rainbow* (Harmondsworth: Penguin, 1950), p. 458.

[11] *The Novel and the World's Dilemma*, p. 125.

[12] "Virginia Woolf: the Last Phase," pp. 381–387.

[13] *The Art of the Novel*, pp. 328–330.

[14] *Virginia Woolf*, pp. 14–15.

[15] Cf. Conrad's *Heart of Darkness*, where the pattern is very similar.

[16] *Twilight on Parnassus*, pp. 396–397.

[17] *The Novel Today*, pp. 87–90. It should be noticed that Henderson is a Marxist critic: that "the external world" has a special sense for him.

[18] *The Novel and Society*, pp. 192, 204, 256.

[19] Paris: Gallimard, 1927, ii, p. 52.

[20] Delattre, p. 146, says that she first read Proust, in the original, in 1922; her diary confirms this date.

[21] Virginia Woolf evidently never read Bergson: Leonard Woolf assured me in a letter, in 1949, that "Mrs. Woolf did not read a word of Bergson," and that, in spite of the fact that her sister-in-law Mrs. Karin Stephen wrote a book on Bergson (*The Misuse of Mind*, 1922), "I very much doubt that she ever discussed Bergson with Mrs. Stephen." Mr. Woolf also wrote that "I do not think that she was influenced in the slightest degree by Bergson's ideas"; but with this it is hard to agree. If she did not read Bergson himself, she most certainly read Proust; and Bergson's ideas were so popular as to be everywhere around her at second and third hand.

[22] Ridley Ambrose, who dislikes long dinners and who has a habit of quoting aloud passages of verse, is in many ways like the Leslie Stephen who appears in Maitland's *Life and Letters of Leslie Stephen* (London: Duckworth, 1906).

[23] *Hours in a Library*, I (London: Murray, 1917), pp. 20, 61, 155; II (London: Smith, Elder, 1894), p. 154.

[24] *Ibid.*, I, pp. 158–160.

[25] *Ibid.*, II, pp. 270ff.

[26] He looked on facts in art as good; she considered facts detrimental to art. Again, they disagreed as to the merits of Congreve, Sterne, and Emily Brontë.

[27] Maitland's *Life*, p. 314. (The "effeminate" man is Coventry Patmore.)

[28] There is a Hardy-like irony in Rachel's dreaming her future without recognizing it. Moreover, the perspective at the beginning of chapter vii is like Hardy in its minimization of humanity, and the picnic scene is a ruined Elizabethan watchtower. On page 110 a stanza from Hardy appropriate to the novel's theme is quoted. These

are of course superficial resemblances; essentially the book is antithetic to Hardy's standpoint. We might also notice these sentences: "When two people have been married for years they seem to become unconscious of each other's bodily presence so that they move as if alone, speak aloud things which they do not expect to be answered, and in general seem to experience all the comfort of solitude without its loneliness. The joint lives of Ridley and Helen had arrived at this stage of community, and it was often necessary for one or the other to recall with an effort whether a thing had been said or only thought, shared or dreamt in private" (p. 195). These stand out—deliberately, for a double meaning—from their context as a perfect parody of Jane Austen.

²⁹ D. S. Savage, "Virginia Woolf," p. 72.

³⁰ Daiches, p. 22. On page 23 Daiches notes that Virginia Woolf's statement, "We go on perseveringly, conscientiously, constructing our two and thirty chapters after a design which more and more ceases to resemble the vision in our minds," is a criticism of *Night and Day* as well as of her contemporaries' novels; "Modern Fiction," in which this statement appears, was published in 1919.

³¹ The noticeably frequent occurrence of the conjunction "but" in this novel suggests in itself a discrepancy. On pp. 134–135 "but" is used eleven times, for example. Of course "but" would naturally appear a good deal in a novel contrasting two attitudes; but the word appears too often—it becomes distracting. This certainly is an example, on the grammatical level, of the form-content variance throughout the novel.

³² *Virginia Woolf*, p. 22.

³³ New York: Knopf, 1921, pp. 95, 214.

³⁴ *The Death of the Moth*, pp. 106–108.

³⁵ "The Early Novels of Virginia Woolf," p. 108.

³⁶ *The Common Reader*, pp. 207–218. It is perhaps necessary to apologize for quoting again from this forever-being-quoted essay, and for repeating some things about it that have been said often and well; but it is essential to any understanding of Virginia Woolf, and one famous passage in it has been consistently misread and deserves reëxamination.

NOTES TO CHAPTER III

THE REGULATION OF A PERSPECTIVE

(Pages 40–76)

¹ *Virginia Woolf—A Commentary*, p. 51.

² Leonard Woolf, in his "Foreword" to *A Haunted House*, p. 7.

³ See, for example, Blackstone, p. 156.

⁴ *Creative Evolution*, translated by Arthur Mitchell (New York: Holt, 1911), p. 181.

⁵ Cf. the image in *The Voyage Out*, p. 109.

⁶ *Creative Evolution*, p. 212.

⁷ In *The Death of the Moth*.

⁸ Karin Stephen, *The Misuse of Mind: a Study of Bergson's Attack on Intellectualism* (New York: Harcourt, Brace, 1922), p. 104.

⁹ It should be noted that explications of Bergson's concepts—even his own explications of them—are always contradictory and confusing. Mrs. Stephen says that "Bergson *must* use self-contradictory terms if the explanation of reality which he offers is to be a true one" (p. 13). Bergson felt that the act of explaining duration was an interference with duration and hence a falsification from the beginning. No wonder that Turquet-Milnes could call *Creative Evolution* "the most wonderful poem

the French have latterly produced" (*Modern French Writers—A Study in Bergsonism*, New York: McBride, 1921, p. 51). Bergson's appeal is to the intuition and imagination rather than to the reason: his many similes and metaphors are beautiful, but must not be pressed to logical conclusions; to ask who lit his Roman candle is tempting, but would be a crime against imagination. Perhaps no small part of his appeal was caused by his avoidance of abstraction, generalization and "dry" reasoning.

[10] Frierson, pp. 133–134.

[11] Burgum, p. 126, believes that the shoes symbolize "the careless rejection of intimacy" with his mother. Perhaps Jacob's feeling for his mother and hers for him are suggested here, but the relationship is probably not thus centralized.

[12] *The Twentieth Century Novel*, p. 493.

[13] *Virginia Woolf* (The Rede Lecture), p. 14.

[14] This is not to say that in Virginia Woolf's later novels each character understands each other character; far from it. But the author—the central intelligence—understands each character; and the novels insist that people can—although not easily—understand and communicate with one another, that they can reach something more essential than the "rooms" around them. Thus method and belief are consistent. Novels in which the author uses an omniscient point of view, and at the same time portrays a world in which each individual is essentially isolated from his fellows and cannot reach them, seem self-contradictory insofar as their authors define experience in a form unsuited to the experience itself as they see it.

[15] On this level, the book is of course a comment on the war that had ended four years before its publication.

[16] See Wiget for a study of time in Virginia Woolf's novels.

[17] Cf. *The Voyage Out*.

[18] *Roman*, January, 1951, p. 12.

[19] *Virginia Woolf—A Study*, p. 78.

[20] "Time in the Novels of Virginia Woolf," pp. 187, 189.

[21] In *The Death of the Moth*.

[22] *Virginia Woolf*, p. 142.

[23] Clarissa Dalloway also figures in some of Virginia Woolf's short stories. As Miss Holtby goes on to show, Virginia Woolf was fond of introducing characters from one of her novels into others, though always in minor roles. Thus, for example, Mrs. Hilbery of *Night and Day* and Mrs. Durrant, Clara, Mr. Bowley, and Moll Pratt of *Jacob's Room*, all reappear in *Mrs. Dalloway*.

[24] "Introduction," p. vi.

[25] "Time in the Novels of Virginia Woolf," pp. 189–190.

[26] *Virginia Woolf*, p. 65. See, for example, page 5 of *Mrs. Dalloway*.

[27] In F. C. Green, *The Mind of Proust* (Cambridge: University Press, 1949), p. 300.

[28] "Virginia Woolf," p. 297.

[29] For a more detailed discussion see my analysis of *The Waves*.

[30] June, 1929, pp. 407ff.

[31] Pp. 34–35. Note the resemblance of this simile to Bergson's famous life-matter rocket simile.

[32] *Creative Evolution*, p. 250.

[33] *Le Temps retrouvé*, i, p. 48.

[34] *A Room of One's Own*, p. 192.

[35] "Addison," in *The Common Reader*, p. 141.

[36] "Notes on an Elizabethan Play," *ibid.*, p. 74.

[37] "Walter Sickert," in *The Captain's Death Bed*, p. 177.

[38] "Robinson Crusoe," in *The Common Reader*, p. 53.

[39] For an interesting discussion of Proust's effect on some of Virginia Woolf's novels see Delattre's book, pp. 146ff.

⁴⁰ *Assessment*, p. 131.
⁴¹ *Main Currents in Modern Literature*, p. 173.
⁴² "How It Strikes a Contemporary," *The Common Reader*, p. 325.
⁴³ Marble, *A Study of the Modern Novel*, p. 95.
⁴⁴ *Virginia Woolf*, p. 73.
⁴⁵ June, 1929, p. 411.
⁴⁶ Burgum, *The Novel and the World's Dilemma*, p. 129.
⁴⁷ *Roman*, January, 1951, pp. 10, 12.
⁴⁸ "Introduction" to *Mrs. Dalloway*, p. v.

NOTES TO CHAPTER IV

The Creative Modulation of Perspective

(Pages 77–131)

¹ Gold'enveizer, *Talks with Tolstoi*, pp. 91–94.
² See, for example, Joan Bennett, p. 79, and the *Times Literary Supplement* review of *Night and Day*. It is perfectly in accord with Virginia Woolf's thought that she should ignore or distort the facts: her roses bloom in December, not because she is careless, but because she considers the resulting artistic effect more important than factual accuracy.
³ "Woolf's *To the Lighthouse*," pp. 9, 11.
⁴ *Virginia Woolf*, pp. 103–104.
⁵ *Virginia Woolf*, p. 36.
⁶ "The Lighthouse, Face to Face."
⁷ "Time in the Novels of Virginia Woolf," p. 151.
⁸ Forster, *Virginia Woolf*, p. 28.
⁹ "Leslie Stephen: Cambridge Critic," p. 405. Q. D. Leavis goes far beyond the realm of literary criticism in her statements about Virginia Woolf's work. She praises *To the Lighthouse*, oddly enough, admiring its formal achievement and complex effects, in *Fiction and the Reading Public*.
¹⁰ See pp. 55–57. Mr. Ramsay resembles Leslie Stephen, and Mrs. Ramsay resembles Virginia Woolf's mother. Julia Stephen had seven children; she was, according to Maitland's *Life* of Leslie Stephen, much interested in young people—in their friendships or love makings—and was loved by them in return (p. 323); she was a woman of really astounding beauty; a practical nurse; she died nine years before her husband. ("A photograph taken by M. Loppé in the 'Bear' shows Mrs. Stephen looking out of the window.... That picture became a treasured relic." p. 397.) The very setting of the novel was suggested by the house at St. Ives where young Virginia spent her summers. "It is a shame to leave the place to itself for so long a time as our absence," Stephen wrote, a year before his wife's death (p. 384).
¹¹ Karin Stephen, p. 78.
¹² "The Wild Goose," p. 108.
¹³ *Albertine disparue*, i, p. 74.
¹⁴ There is obviously a more than casual similarity between Mr. Paunceforte and the Edwardian novelists, and between Lily and the Georgians.
¹⁵ *Albertine disparue*, i, p. 100.
¹⁶ R. L. Chambers, *The Novels of Virginia Woolf*, p. 7.
¹⁷ *Roman*, January, 1951, pp. 11–12.
¹⁸ Beach, *The Twentieth Century Novel*, p. 490.

[19] Beck, "For Virginia Woolf," p. 244.

[20] Gallard, review of Holtby's *Virginia Woolf*, p. 351.

[21] Holtby, *Virginia Woolf*, p. 177.

[22] Spender, *World Within World*, pp. 137–138.

[23] *Virginia Woolf—A Study*, p. 17.

[24] *Creative Evolution*, pp. 258, 268.

[25] *Le Roman*, p. 172.

[26] *Creative Evolution*, p. 267.

[27] See Delattre, pp. 172ff., and Wiget, p. 66. I am grateful to Alvin A. Eustis of the University of California for mentioning to me the ever so much more interesting similarity of *Orlando* to Gautier's *Mademoiselle De Maupin*.

[28] See, for example, pp. 70, 161, 162–163, 164, 172–173.

[29] This might be seen as echoing, unintentionally of course, Nick Greene's contempt for the Elizabethan poets.

[30] Pp. 97ff., especially p. 99. Cf. *Three Guineas* and *A Room of One's Own*.

[31] P. 37; this can also be seen, of course, in *The Voyage Out* and *Mrs. Dalloway*.

[32] P. 189. Cf. "Why?" in *The Death of the Moth*.

[33] *Le Temps retrouvé*, ii, p. 39.

[34] Pp. 178, 180.

[35] B. Ifor Evans remarks that "if only the exuberance of [the Great Frost] passage could have entered her other work, uniting itself with a physical vitality which gave her a zest for all types of experience, she would have become one of the greatest of English novelists." He adds that *Between the Acts* comes closest to uniting *Orlando's* "historical pagentry and colour" with the novels' insight and "profundity of vision" (*English Literature between the Wars*, p. 74).

[36] *Le Temps retrouvé*, ii, p. 244.

[37] *Creative Evolution*, p. 271.

[38] See, for example, Graham, p. 195; Daiches, pp. 109–110.

[39] "Virginia Woolf," p. 299n.

[40] *The Novel and the World's Dilemma*, p. 135.

[41] "Mrs. Woolf and Life," p. 380.

[42] *The Novel and Society*, p. 208.

[43] "Virginia Woolf," p. 97.

[44] "Modernism," p. 675.

[45] *Some Studies in the Modern Novel*, p. 63. The allusions to Eliot's poetry serve to enrich *The Waves* insofar as it reviews and confirms, instead of only stating, what the contemporary intellect has made of experience: the characters of *The Waste Land* have problems in common with the speakers in *The Waves*, although none of the former is able to solve them, and only Tiresias to transcend them by understanding them.

[46] "The Lighthouse, Face to Face," p. 122.

[47] *Virginia Woolf*, p. 47.

[48] *Virginia Woolf—A Commentary*, p. 169.

[49] See William Troy, "Virginia Woolf." Cf. Dorothy Hoare, *Some Studies in the Modern Novel;* N. Elizabeth Monroe, *The Novel and Society;* Philip Toynbee, "Virginia Woolf"; the critics Leavis, et al.

[50] "Manners, Morals, and the Novel," in *Forms of Fiction*, ed. W. Van O'Connor (Minneapolis: University of Minnesota Press, 1948), p. 150.

[51] Delattre, p. 206.

[52] *The Common Reader*, p. 237.

[53] P. 134.

[54] "Phases of Fiction," June, pp. 411–412.

[55] *Talks with Tolstoi*, p. 81. Still another attitude is T. S. Eliot's; in *"Ulysses,* Order,

and Myth," he writes, "I am not begging the question in calling *Ulysses* a 'novel'; and if you call it an epic it will not matter. If it is not a novel, that is simply because the novel, instead of being a form, was simply the expression of an age which had not sufficiently lost all form to feel the need of something stricter.... The novel ended with Flaubert and with James" (in *Forms of Fiction*, p. 123).

[56] "Mr. Bennett and Mrs. Brown," in *The Captain's Death Bed*, p. 106.

[57] *The Novels of Virginia Woolf*, pp. 76, 94.

[58] *The English Novel in Transition*, p. 317.

[59] *Tendencies of the Modern Novel*, p. 16.

[60] W. Y. Tindall, "Introduction" to Lawrence's *The Plumed Serpent* (New York: Knopf, 1951).

[61] M. Widdows, "Virginia Woolf," *Annual Register*, 1941; quoted in Chambers, p. 60.

[62] William Plomer, "Virginia Woolf," p. 326.

[63] *Nouvelle Revue Française*, May 1, 1927, pp. 669–675.

[64] *The Art of the Novel*, ed. R. P. Blackmur (New York: Scribner's, 1934), p. 290.

NOTES TO CHAPTER V

The Last Novels

(Pages 132–161)

[1] Savage, p. 100.

[2] W. Troy, "Variations on a Theme," p. 474. This seems a meaningless comment, and the value judgment it suggests is not substantiated: Shakespeare's tragedies could also be called "formal variations upon the same old ... tune," for example.

[3] *Virginia Woolf und die Konzeption der Zeit in ihren Werken*, p. 93.

[4] *Virginia Quarterly Review*, Summer, 1937, pp. 437–439.

[5] "Mrs. Woolf and Life," p. 380. (Cf. *The Years*, p. 184.) Mellers' statement that "the complete omission, in a work which embraces the passage of time during the last fifty years, of (for example) physical desire may strike us at least as odd," is itself odd: in the very first sequence, and throughout the novel, physical desire is dealt with both explicitly and implicitly.

[6] Karin Stephen, p. 102.

[7] *Creative Evolution*, pp. 263–264.

[8] Savage, "Virginia Woolf," p. 100.

[9] Daiches, Virginia Woolf, p. 120.

[10] See, for example, Daiches, pp. 111–112; Delattre, "Le Nouveau roman de Virginia Woolf," pp. 289ff.

[11] *The Forsyte Saga* (New York: Scribner's, 1934), pp. 59, 61.

[12] *Man and Superman*, in *Selected Plays*, III (New York: Dodd, Mead, 1948), p. 646.

[13] Sympathetic as well as adverse critics hold this opinion; see, for example, Deborah Newton, pp. 54–55; Chambers, p. 46.

[14] *Virginia Woolf*, p. 17.

[15] *Virginia Woolf, Her Art as a Novelist*, p. 113.

[16] "Time in the Novels of Virginia Woolf," p. 200.

[17] *Creative Evolution*, p. 261.

[18] This is of course the central problem of Bergson's *Time and Free Will* (*Essai sur les données immédiates de la conscience*).

[19] Karin Stephen, p. 78.

[20] James S. Wilson, "Time and Virginia Woolf," p. 274.

[21] P. 233. It can be noticed how much more than "Bergsonistic" is this idea, and the perspective of the novel as a whole.

[22] "For Virginia Woolf," p. 252. This essay demonstrates "that introspectiveness in her novels was not wilfully esoteric or uncritically glorified, and that she did interrelate subjective individualism and the social order." Beck sees Isa, Mrs. Swithin, and Miss La Trobe as facets of the English mind.

[23] Bergson, *Time and Free Will*, in D. B. Kitchen, *Bergson for Beginners* (London: G. Allen, 1914), p. 176.

[24] Chambers thinks the pageant a "despedate artistic shift" to which Virginia Woolf was put to express a "message" (*The Novels of Virginia Woolf*, p. 50); and D. S. Savage thinks the pageant "moronic" ("Virginia Woolf," p. 103).

[25] "Virginia Woolf's Last Novel," p. 344. Cf. the interpretation of H. V. Routh, who feels that *Between the Acts*, "despite the guesses which have been made at a hidden meaning, can most safely be read as a piece of genial, local satire" (*English Literature and Ideas in the Twentieth Century*, p. 175).

[26] "Mrs. Woolf and Mrs. Brown," p. 140. Bernard Blackstone mentions early in his book that "the mastery of technique falters in Between the Acts" (p. 149), but his chapter on this novel has no trace of the idea.

[27] Beck, "For Virginia Woolf"; Joan Bennett, *Virginia Woolf, Her Art as a Novelist*, pp. 112–131.

[28] *Reading a Novel*, p. 44.

[29] "Time and Virginia Woolf," p. 273.

[30] "How It Strikes a Contemporary," *The Common Reader*, p. 332.

NOTES TO CHAPTER VI

Conclusion

(Pages 162–167)

[1] Earl Daniels, *"The Waves,"* p. 352.

[2] "The Novels of George Meredith," *The Common Reader*, pp. 247–248, 253.

[3] N. Elizabeth Monroe, *The Novel and Society*, p. 224.

[4] Wilson, "Time and Virginia Woolf," p. 273.

[5] "The Novels of E. M. Forster," p. 107.

[6] Intermission talk on a broadcast of *Mrs. Dalloway*.

[7] George Santayana, *Winds of Doctrine* (New York: Scribner's, 1913), p. 107.

[8] Beck, "For Virginia Woolf," p. 253.

BIBLIOGRAPHY

BIBLIOGRAPHY

By Virginia Woolf

Virginia Woolf's works are published in England by the Hogarth Press, and in the United States by Harcourt, Brace and Company. Editions here are those to which reference is made in this study.

NOVELS

Between the Acts. London: Hogarth Press, 1947.
Jacob's Room. New York: Harcourt, Brace, 1923.
Mrs. Dalloway. New York: Modern Library, 1928.
Night and Day. London: Hogarth Press, 1950.
Orlando. A Biography. New York: Penguin Books, Inc., 1946.
To the Lighthouse. New York: Harcourt, Brace, 1927.
The Voyage Out. New York: Harcourt, Brace, 1920.
The Waves. New York: Harcourt, Brace, 1931.
The Years. New York: Harcourt, Brace, 1937.

SHORT STORIES

A Haunted House. London: Hogarth Press, 1947.
Monday or Tuesday. New York: Harcourt, Brace, 1921.
Two Stories (with Leonard Woolf). London: Hogarth Press, 1917.

CRITICISM AND SKETCHES

The Captain's Death Bed and Other Essays. London: Hogarth Press, 1950.
The Common Reader (First and Second Series Combined). New York: Harcourt, Brace, 1948.
The Death of the Moth and Other Essays. New York: Harcourt, Brace, 1932.
The Moment and Other Essays. New York: Harcourt, Brace, 1948.
A Room of One's Own. New York: Harcourt, Brace, 1929.
Street Haunting. San Francisco: Westgate Press, 1930.
Three Guineas. London: Hogarth Press, 1938.
"Phases of Fiction." *Bookman,* April, 1929, pp. 123–132; May, 1929, pp. 269–279; June, 1929, pp. 404–412.
"Women and Fiction." *Forum,* March, 1929, pp. 179–183.

BIOGRAPHY

Flush: A Biography. New York: Harcourt, Brace, 1933.
Roger Fry: A Biography. New York: Harcourt, Brace, 1940.

INTRODUCTIONS

"Introduction." *By the Ionian Sea,* by George Gissing. London: Cape, 1933.
"Introductory Letter to Margaret Llewelyn Davies." *Life as We Have Known It, by Co-operative Working Women,* ed. M. L. Davies. London: L. and V. Woolf, 1931.
"Introduction." *Mrs. Dalloway.* New York: Modern Library, 1928.
"Introduction." *A Sentimental Journey through France and Italy,* by Laurence Sterne. Oxford: University Press, 1928.
"Julia Margaret Cameron." *Victorian Photographs of Famous Men and Fair Women,* by Mrs. J. Cameron. London: L. and V. Woolf, 1926.

[183]

TRANSLATIONS

(With S. S. Koteliansky)

Dostoevskii, F. M. *Stavrogin's Confession and the Plan of the Life of a Great Sinner.* Richmond, England: L. and V. Woolf, 1922.

Gold'enveizer, A. B. *Talks with Tolstoi.* Richmond, England: L. and V. Woolf, 1923.

Tolstoi, L. H. *Tolstoi's Love Letters, with a Study on the Autobiographical Elements in Tolstoi's Work by P. Beryukov.* Richmond, England: L. and V. Woolf, 1923.

DIARY

"Le Journal inédit de Virginia Woolf." *Roman,* Jan., 1951, pp. 9–13 (selections from 1925–1927, translated by Rose Celli).

A Writer's Diary. London: Hogarth Press, 1953.

ABOUT VIRGINIA WOOLF

Aiken, Conrad. Review of *Orlando. Dial,* Feb., 1929, pp. 147–149.

Allen, Walter. *Reading a Novel.* London: Phoenix House, 1949, pp. 40–43.

Annan, Noel G. *Leslie Stephen. His Thought and Character in Relation to His Time.* London: Macgibbon and Kee, 1951.

Arrowsmith, J. E. S. Review of *The Waves. Mercury,* Dec., 1931, pp. 204–205.

Badenhausen, I. *Die Sprache Virginia Woolfs. Ein Beitrag zur Stilistik des modernen englischen Romans.* Marburg: Ebel, 1932.

Badt-Strauss, B. "Das Werk der Virginia Woolf." *Die Literatur,* 1932, pp. 607–609.

Beach, J. W. "Virginia Woolf." *English Journal,* Oct., 1937, pp. 603–612.

Beck, Warren. "For Virginia Woolf." *Forms of Modern Fiction,* ed. W. Van O'Connor. Minneapolis: University of Minnesota Press, 1948, pp. 243–253.

Bell, Clive. "Virginia Woolf." *Dial,* Dec., 1924, pp. 451–465.

Bennett, Arnold. *The Savour of Life. Essays in Gusto.* London: Cassell, 1928, pp. 47–49 *et passim.*

Bennett, Joan. "Le Journal inédit de Virginia Woolf." *Roman,* Jan., 1951, pp. 6–8.

———. *Virginia Woolf, Her Art as a Novelist.* Cambridge: University Press, 1945.

Bizé, Paul. "Virginia Woolf as a Literary Artist." (Mémoire présenté à la Faculté des Lettres de Lille, pour le diplôme d'Études supérieures d'anglais), July, 1930.

Blackstone, Bernard. *Virginia Woolf: a Commentary.* New York: Harcourt, Brace, 1949.

Blanche, Jacques-Émile. Review of *Orlando. Les Nouvelles Littéraires,* Feb. 16, 1929, p. 9.

Brace, M. "Worshipping Solid Objects: the Pagan World of Virginia Woolf." *Accent Anthology,* New York: Harcourt, Brace, 1946, pp. 489–495.

Bradbrook, M. C. "Notes on the Style of Mrs. Woolf." *Scrutiny,* May, 1932, pp. 33–38.

Brewster, D., and A. Burrell. "The Wild Goose: Virginia Woolf's Pursuit of Life." *Adventure or Experience.* New York: Columbia University Press, 1930, pp. 77–116.

Bullett, Gerald. Review of *Mrs. Dalloway. Saturday Review,* May 30, 1925, p. 588.

———. Review of *Orlando. English Journal,* Dec., 1928, pp. 793–800.

Burgum, E. B. "Virginia Woolf and the Empty Room." *The Novel and the World's Dilemma.* New York: Oxford University Press, 1947, pp. 120–139.

Burra, P. "Virginia Woolf." *Nineteenth Century,* Jan., 1934, pp. 512–525.

C., F. X. Review of *The Years. Catholic World,* July, 1937, pp. 501–502.

Canby, H. S. Review of *Orlando. Saturday Review of Literature,* Nov. 3, 1928, pp. 313–314.

Carew, Dudley. "Virginia Woolf." *Mercury,* May, 1926, pp. 40–49.

Cecil, Lord David. "Two Twentieth-Century Novelists: Virginia Woolf and E. M. Forster." *Poets and Story-tellers.* London: Constable, 1949, pp. 153–201.

Chambers, R. *The Novels of Virginia Woolf*. Edinburgh: Oliver and Boyd, 1947.

Chastaing, M. *La Philosophie de Virginia Woolf*. Paris: Presses Universitaires, 1951.

Daiches, David. "Virginia Woolf." *The Novel and the Modern World*. Chicago: Univeristy of Chicago Press, 1939, pp. 158–187.

——. *Virginia Woolf*. Norfolk, Conn.: New Directions, 1942.

Daniel-Rops. "Une Technique nouvelle: le monologue intérieur." *Correspondent*, Jan. 25, 1932, pp. 281–305.

Daniels, Earl. "*The Waves.*" *Saturday Review of Literature*, Dec. 5, 1931, p. 352.

Delattre, Floris. "La Durée bergsonienne dans le roman de Virginia Woolf." *Revue Anglo-Américaine*, Dec., 1931, pp. 97–108.

——. "Le Nouveau roman de Virginia Woolf." *Études Anglaises*, July, 1937, pp. 289–298.

——. *Le Roman psychologique de Virginia Woolf*. Paris: Librarie Philosophique J. Krin, 1932.

Dottin, P. "Les Sortilèges de Mrs Virginia Woolf." *Revue de France*, April 1, 1930, pp. 556–566.

Eliot, T. S. "Virginia Woolf." *Horizon*, May, 1941, pp. 313–316.

Elkan, L. "Virginia Woolf, ihre kunstlerische Idee und ihre Auffassung der Form." *Der Kreis* (Hamburg), 1931, pp. 148–152.

Empson, William. "Virginia Woolf." *Scrutinies, Vol. II*, ed. Edgell Rickword. London: Wishart, 1931, pp. 203–216.

Eshelman, L. W. Review of *The Years*. *Commonweal*, July 23, 1937, p. 329.

Finke, I. "Virginia Woolfs Stellung zur Wirklichkeit." (Marburg dissertation), 1933.

Forster, E. M. "The Early Novels of Virginia Woolf." *Abinger Harvest*. New York: Harcourt, Brace, 1936, pp. 106–115.

——. *Virginia Woolf* (Rede Lecture, May 29, 1941). Cambridge: University Press, 1942.

Gallard, R. Review of *Le Roman psychologique de Virginia Woolf* by F. Delattre. *Revue Anglo-Américaine*, Dec., 1932, pp. 158–160.

——. Review of *Virginia Woolf* by W. Holtby. *Revue Anglo-Américaine*, April, 1933, pp. 350–352.

Garnett, David. "Virginia Woolf." *New Statesman and Nation*, April 12, 1941, p. 386.

Genêt. "Letter from Paris, March 29." *The New Yorker*, April 7, 1951, pp. 70–74.

Gillet, L. Review of *Orlando*. *Revue des Deux Mondes*, Sept. 1, 1929, pp. 218–230.

Gould, Gerald. Review of *The Voyage Out*. *New Statesman*, April 10, 1915, pp. 18–19.

Graham, John. "Time in the Novels of Virginia Woolf." *University of Toronto Quarterly*, Jan., 1949, pp. 186–201.

Grant, Duncan. "Virginia Woolf." *Horizon*, June, 1941, pp. 402–406.

Gruber, Ruth. *Virginia Woolf—A Study*. Leipzig: Tauchnitz, 1936.

Hartley, Lodwick. "Of Time and Mrs. Woolf." *Sewanee Review*, April–June, 1939, pp. 235–241.

——. Review of *The Waves*. *South Atlantic Quarterly*, July, 1932, pp. 349–351.

Harwood, H. C. "Recent Tendencies in Modern Fiction." *Quarterly Review*, April, 1929, pp. 321–338.

——. Review of *The Waves*. *Saturday Review*, Oct. 10, 1931, p. 462.

Herrick, Robert. "The Works of Mrs. Woolf." *Saturday Review of Literature*, Dec. 5, 1931, p. 346.

Heuer, H. Review of *Die Sprache Virginia Woolfs* by I. Badenhausen. *Anglia Beiblatt*, Feb., 1934, pp. 61–63.

Hicks, G. Review of *The Years*. *New Republic*, April 28, 1937, p. 363.

Hoare, Dorothy. "Virginia Woolf." *Some Studies in the Modern Novel*. London: Chatto and Windus, 1936, pp. 36–67.

——. "Virginia Woolf." *Cambridge Review*, Oct. 16, 1931, pp. 27–28.

Holtby, Winifred. *Virginia Woolf.* London: Wishart, 1932.
Humphrey, Mary C. Review of *To the Lighthouse. Virginia Quarterly Review,* Jan., 1928, pp. 119ff.
Impressions (Paris), Jan., 1938.
Jack, P. M. Review of *The Years. New York Herald Tribune Book Review,* April 11, 1937, pp. 1, 27.
Jameson, Storm. Review of *The Waves. Fortnightly Review,* Nov., 1931, pp. 677–678.
Johnson, R. B. *Some Women Novelists.* London: L. Parsons, 1922 (see especially pp. 149–160).
Josephson, Matthew. "Virginia Woolf and the Modern Novel." *New Republic,* April 15, 1931, pp. 239–241.
K., F. W. Review of *To the Lighthouse. Sewanee Review,* July–Sept., 1927, pp. 364–366.
Kelsey, Mary E. "Virginia Woolf and the She-Condition." *Sewanee Review,* Oct.–Dec., 1931, pp. 425–444.
Kronenberger, Louis. "Virginia Woolf's Last Novel." *Nation,* Oct. 11, 1941, pp. 344–345.
Kunitz, S. J., and H. Haycraft. *Twentieth Century Authors.* New York: H. W. Wilson, 1942, pp. 1548–1550.
Lady Oxford. "Tribute." *London Times,* April 9, 1941, p. 7.
Lalou, René. "La Sentiment de l'unité humaine chez Virginia Woolf et Aldous Huxley." *Europe,* Oct. 15, 1937, pp. 266–272.
Lanoire, N. "Le Témoignage de Mrs Dalloway." *Les Lettres,* June, 1930, pp. 81–91.
Lawrence, Margaret. "Virginia Woolf." *School of Femininity.* New York: Frederick Stokes, 1936, pp. 373–382.
Leavis, Q. D. "Caterpillars of the Commonwealth Unite!" *The Importance of Scrutiny,* ed. Eric Bentley. New York: George W. Stewart, 1948, pp. 382–391.
Lehmann, John. "Virginia Woolf." *The Open Night.* London: Longmans Green, 1952, pp. 23–33.
Lohmüller, G. "Die Frau im Werk von Virginia Woolf." (Tübingen dissertation), 1937.
Macaulay, Rose. "Virginia Woolf." *Horizon,* May, 1941, pp. 316–318.
Mais, Stuart P. B. *Why We Should Read* ———. New York: Dodd, Mead, 1921.
Marcel, Gabriel. Review of *The Waves. Nouvelle Revue Française,* Feb., 1932, pp. 303–308.
Masui, J. "Virginia Woolf." *Le Flambeau* (Brussels), Jan., 1932, pp. 78–95.
Maurois, André. "Préface" to *Mrs. Dalloway,* translated by S. David. Paris: Stock, 1929.
———. "Première rencontre avec Virginia Woolf." *Les Nouvelles Littéraires,* Jan. 19, 1929, p. 1.
Mauron, Charles. "Préface" to *Orlando,* translated by C. Mauron. Paris: Stock, 1931.
Mayoux, J-J. "A Propos d'*Orlando* de Virginia Woolf." *Europe,* Jan., 1930, pp. 117–122.
———. "Le Roman de l'espace et du temps: Virginia Woolf." *Revue Anglo-Américaine,* April, 1930, pp. 312–326.
———. Review of *To the Lighthouse. Revue Anglo-Américaine,* June, 1928, pp. 424–438.
Mellers, W. H. "Mrs. Woolf and Life." *The Importance of Scrutiny,* ed. Eric Bentley. New York: George W. Stewart, 1948, pp. 378–382.
———. "Virginia Woolf: the Last Phase." *Kenyon Review,* Autumn, 1942, pp. 381–387.
Mendilow, A. A. *Time and the Novel.* London: Peter Nevill, 1952.
Morra, Umberto. "Il nuovo romanzo inglese: Virginia Woolf." *La Cultura,* Jan., 1931, pp. 34–51.

Mortimer, Raymond. "Mrs. Woolf and Mr. Strachey." *American Bookman*, Feb., 1929, pp. 625–629.

"Mrs. Woolf on Leslie Stephen." *American Bookman*, Feb., 1933, pp. 154–155.

"Mrs. Woolf's Death." *Time*, April 14, 1941, pp. 34, 36.

"Mrs. Woolf's New Novel." *Times Literary Supplement*, Oct. 8, 1931, p. 773.

Muir, Edwin. "Virginia Woolf." *American Bookman*, Dec., 1931, pp. 362–367.

———. "Virginia Woolf." *Nation-Athenaeum*, April 17, 1926, pp. 70–72.

Muller, Herbert J. "Virginia Woolf and Feminine Fiction." *Saturday Review of Literature*, Feb. 6, 1937, pp. 3–4, 14, 16. (Cf. E. W. Cogswell, *ibid.*, Feb. 20, 1937, p. 9.)

Newton, Deborah. *Virginia Woolf*. Melbourne: University of Melbourne Press, 1946.

"Night and Day." *Times Literary Supplement*, Oct. 30, 1919, p. 607.

"A Novelist's Experiment." *Times Literary Supplement*, May 21, 1925, p. 349.

Occampo, Victoria. *Virginia Woolf, Orlando y Cía*. Buenos Aires: SUR, 1938.

"Orlando." *Life and Letters*, Nov. 1, 1928, pp. 514–516.

"Orlando." *Times Literary Supplement*, Oct. 11, 1928, p. 729.

Overcarsh, F. L. "The Lighthouse, Face to Face." *Accent*, Winter, 1950, pp. 107–123.

Peel, Robert. "Virginia Woolf." *New Criterion*, Oct., 1933, pp. 78–96.

Plomer, William. "Virginia Woolf." *Horizon*, May, 1941, pp. 323–327.

Porter, Katherine Anne. Intermission talk on broadcast of *Mrs. Dalloway* in play form ("NBC Theatre," April 3, 1950).

Rahv, Philip. "Mrs. Woolf and Mrs. Brown." *Image and Idea*. Norfolk, Conn.: New Directions, 1949, pp. 139–143.

Reade, A. R. "Experiment and Virginia Woolf." *Main Currents in Modern Literature*. London: Ivor Nicholson and Watson Ltd., 1935, pp. 165–178.

Rey, Jean. "The Evolution of Mrs. Woolf's Technique and Style." (Mémoire présenté à la Faculté des Lettres de Lille, pour le Diplôme d'Études supérieures d'anglais), Nov., 1930.

Rillo, Lila E. *Katherine Mansfield . . . and Virginia Woolf. . . .* Buenos Aires: Talleras gráficos Contreras, 1944.

Roberts, J. H. "Toward Virginia Woolf." *Virginia Quarterly Review*, Oct., 1934, pp. 587–602.

———. " 'Vision and Design' in Virginia Woolf." *PMLA*, 1946, pp. 835–847.

Roberts, R. E. "Virginia Woolf." *Bookman*, Jan., 1928, pp. 220–221.

Rosati, Salvatore. "Virginia Woolf." *English Miscellany*, 1 (Rome, 1950), pp. 145–159.

Russell, H. K. "Woolf's *To the Lighthouse*." *The Explicator*, March, 1950, pp. 9, 11.

Sackville-West, Victoria. "Virginia Woolf." *Horizon*, May, 1941, pp. 318–323.

St. Jean, E. de. Review of *Mrs. Dalloway*. *Revue Hebdomadaire*, March 16, 1929, pp. 363–367.

Sanna, Vittoria. *Il Romanzo di Virginia Woolf; Inspirazione e Motivi Fondamentali*. Florence: Marsocco, 1951.

Savage, D. S. "Virginia Woolf." *The Withered Branch—Six Studies in the Modern Novel*. London: Eyre and Spottiswood, 1950, pp. 70–105.

———. "The Mind of Virginia Woolf." *South Atlantic Quarterly*, Oct., 1947, pp. 556–573.

Segura, Celia. "The Transcendental and the Transitory in Virginia Woolf's Novels." *Two Studies in the Contemporary Novel* (A. Jehin and C. Segura). Buenos Aires: Talleras gráficos Contreras, 1943.

Sir Galahad. "Virginia Woolf." *Neue Schweizer Rundschau*, 1948, pp. 528–541.

Sitwell, Edith. "Virginia Woolf." *English Women*. London: William Collins, 1942, pp. 47–48.

Snow, Lotus A. "Imagery in Virginia Woolf's Novels." University of Chicago (unpublished dissertation), 1949.

Stallman, R. W. "Virginia Woolf" (bibliography). *Critiques and Essays on Modern Fiction 1920–51*, ed. J. W. Aldridge. New York: Ronald Press, 1952, pp. 608–610.

Stephen, Adrian. *The "Dreadnought" Hoax*. London: Hogarth Press, 1936.

Strong, L. A. G. Review of *The Waves. Spectator,* Oct. 10, 1931, pp. 468, 470.

Sudrann, Jean. "The Sea, the City and the Clock; a Study of Symbolic Form in the Novels of Virginia Woolf." Columbia University (unpublished dissertation), 1951.

"A Suicide Note." *Time,* May 5, 1941, p. 97.

Swinnerton, Frank. "Mrs. Woolf Again." *A London Bookman.* London: Martin Secker, 1930, pp. 147–153.

———. "Mrs. Woolf on the Novel." *A London Bookman.* London: Martin Secker, 1930, pp. 111–118.

Sykes, Gerald. "Modernism." *Nation,* Dec. 16, 1931, pp. 674–675.

Tante, Dilly (pseud. S. J. Kunitz), ed. *Living Authors.* New York: H. W. Wilson Co., 1931. "Virginia Woolf," pp. 448–450.

Toerien, B. J. *A Bibliography of Virginia Woolf . . .* Cape Town, 1943.

"To the Lighthouse." *Times Literary Supplement,* May 5, 1927, p. 315.

Toynbee, Philip. "Virginia Woolf." *Horizon,* Nov., 1946, pp. 290–304.

Troy, William. "Variations on a Theme." *Nation,* April 24, 1937, pp. 473–474.

———. "Virginia Woolf. 1: The Poetic Method; 2: The Poetic Style." *Symposium,* Jan., 1932, pp. 53–63; April, 1932, pp. 153–166.

"The Voyage Out." *Times Literary Supplement,* April 1, 1915, p. 110.

Walpole, Hugh. "Virginia Woolf." *New Statesman and Nation,* June 14, 1941, pp. 602–603.

Weidner, E. "Impressionismus und Expressionismus in den Romanen Virginia Woolfs." (Griefswald dissertation), 1934.

White, E. W. "Virginia Woolf." *Die Weltbühne,* 1929, pp. 18–20.

Wiget, Erik. *Virginia Woolf und die Konzeption der Zeit in ihren Werken.* Zurich: Juris-Verlag, 1949.

Williams, Orlo. Review of *To the Lighthouse. New Criterion,* July, 1927, pp. 74–78.

———. Review of *The Years. New Criterion,* July, 1937, pp. 714–716.

Wilson, James S. "Time and Virginia Woolf." *Virginia Quarterly Review,* Spring, 1942, pp. 267–276.

"The Years." *Times Literary Supplement,* March 13, 1937, p. 185.

General

Beach, J. W. *The Twentieth Century Novel, Studies in Technique.* New York and London: Appleton-Century-Crofts, 1932.

Blumenthal, Margrete. *Zur Technik des englischen Gegenwartsromans.* Leipzig: Tauchnitz, 1935.

Bowen, Elizabeth. *English Novelists.* London: William Collins, 1942.

Bowling, L. M. "Dramatizing the Mind: a Study of 'Stream of Consciousness' Technique." (University of Iowa dissertation.) 1946.

Brewster, D., and A. Burrell. *Modern Fiction.* New York: Columbia University Press, 1934.

Bullett, Gerald. *Modern English Fiction.* A Personal View. London: H. Jenkins, 1926.

Carruthers, John (pseud. John Y. T. Craig). *Scheherazade, or the Future of the English Novel.* London: K. Paul, Trench, Trubner, 1927.

Cazamian, L., and E. Legouis. *Histoire de la littérature anglaise.* Paris: Hochette, 1924.

Charques, R. D. *Contemporary Literature and Social Revolution.* London: Martin Secker, 1933.

Chevalley, Abel. *Le Roman anglais de notre temps.* London: H. H. Milford, 1921.

Church, Richard. *British Authors.* London: Longmans Green, 1948.
———. *The Growth of the English Novel.* London: Methuen, 1951.
Collins, A. S. *English Literature of the Twentieth Century.* London: University Tutorial Press, 1951.
Collins, Joseph. *The Doctor Looks at Literature. Psychological Studies of Life and Letters.* London and New York: George H. Doran, 1928.
Collins, Norman. *The Facts of Fiction.* London: V. Gollancz, 1932.
Comfort, Alex. *The Novel of Our Time.* Denver: Swallow, 1949.
Connolly, Cyril. *The Condemned Playground.* New York: Macmillan, 1946.
———. *Enemies of Promise.* New York: Macmillan, 1948.
Courtney, Janet E. *The Women of My Time.* London: L. Dickson, 1934.
Cunliffe, J. W. *English Literature in the Twentieth Century.* New York: Macmillan, 1933.
Dobrée, Bonamy. *Modern Prose Style.* Oxford: Clarendon, 1934.
Drew, Elizabeth. *Some Aspects of Contemporary Fiction.* New York: Harcourt, Brace, 1926.
Edgar, Pelham. *The Art of the Novel from 1700 to the Present Time.* New York: Macmillan, 1933.
Eliot, T. S. "Le Roman anglais contemporain." *Nouvelle Revue Française,* May 1, 1927, pp. 669–675.
Ellis, G. U. *Twilight on Parnassus: a Survey of Post-War Fiction and Pre-War Criticism.* London: Michael Joseph, 1939.
Evans, B. Ifor. *English Literature between the Wars.* London: Methuen, 1948.
Fehr, Bernhard. *Die englische Literatur der Gegenwart und die Kulturfragen unserer Zeit.* Leipzig: Tauchnitz, 1931.
———. *Englische Prosa von 1880 bis zur Gegenwart.* Leipzig: Tauchnitz, 1927.
Forster, E. M. *Aspects of the Novel.* New York: Harcourt, Brace, 1927.
Fraser, G. S. "The Revival of Romance." *English Review,* July, 1935, pp. 23–30.
Frierson, F. C. *The English Novel in Transition 1885–1940.* Norman: University of Oklahoma Press, 1942.
George, W. L. "A Painter's Literature." *English Review,* March, 1920, pp. 223–234.
Gillet, Louis. *Esquisses anglaises.* Paris: Firmin Didot, 1930.
Gillett, Eric W. *Books and Writers.* Singapore, Straits Settlements: Malaya Publishing House, 1930.
Gould, Gerald. *The English Novel of Today.* London: John Castle, 1924.
Grabo, Carl H. *The Technique of the Novel.* New York: Scribner's, 1928.
Graves, R., and A. Hodge. *The Long Week-End; a Social History of Great Britain 1918–1939.* New York: Macmillan, 1941.
Harrod, R. F. *The Life of John Maynard Keynes.* New York: Harcourt, Brace, 1951.
Hawkins, E. W. "The Stream of Consciousness Novel." *Atlantic Monthly,* Sept., 1926, pp. 356–360.
Heard, Gerald. *These Hurrying Years, an Historical Outline, 1900–1933.* London: Chatto and Windus, 1934.
Henderson, Philip. *The Novel Today.* London: John Lane, 1936.
Isaacs, J. *An Assessment of Twentieth-Century Literature.* London: Secker and Warburg, 1951.
Jaloux, Edmund. *Au Pays du roman.* Paris: R. A. Corrêa, 1931.
Jameson, Storm. "The Georgian Novel and Mr. Robinson." *Bookman,* July, 1929, pp. 449–463.
———. *The Novel in Contemporary Life.* Boston: The Writer, 1939.
Kettle, Arnold. *An Introduction to the English Novel,* Vol. II. London: Hutchinson's University Library, 1953.

Knight, Grant C. *The Novel in English*. New York: Richard R. Smith, 1931.

Lalou, René. *Littérature anglaise* (Panorama des littératures contemporaines). Paris: Kra, 1926.

Leavis, F. R. Review of *Two Memoirs* by J. M. Keynes. *Scrutiny*, Sept., 1949, pp. 243–246.

Leavis, Q. D. *Fiction and the Reading Public*. London: Chatto and Windus, 1932.

———. "Leslie Stephen: Cambridge Critic." *Scrutiny*, March, 1939, pp. 404–415.

Linati, Carlo. *Scrittori anglo-americani d'oggi*. Milan: Corticelli, 1932.

Logé, Marc. "Quelques romancières anglaises contemporaines." *Revue Bleue*, Nov. 21, 1925, pp. 753–756.

Lovett, R. M., and H. S. Hughes. *The History of the Novel in England*. Boston: Houghton Mifflin, 1932.

Mackenzie, Compton. *Literature in My Time*. London: Rich and Cowan, 1933.

Mais, Stuart P. B. *Some Modern Authors*. New York: Dodd, Mead, 1923.

Mansfield, K. *Novels and Novelists*. London: Constable, 1930.

Marble, A. R. *A Study of the Modern Novel*. New York: Appleton, 1928.

Maurois, A. *Quatre études anglaises*. Paris: B. Grasset, 1927.

Millett, Fred B. *Contemporary British Literature, a Critical Survey and 232 Author-Bibliographies*. New York: Harcourt, Brace, 1935 (3d ed., based on 2d ed. by J. M. Manly and E. Rickert).

Monroe, N. Elizabeth. *The Novel and Society—a Critical Study of the Modern Novel*. Chapel Hill: University of North Carolina Press, 1941. ("Experimental Humanism in Virginia Woolf," pp. 188–224.)

Moore, R. W. *Prose at Present*. London: Bell, 1933.

Morrow, Christine. *Le Roman irréaliste dans les littératures contemporaines de langues française et anglaise*. Paris: Didier, 1941.

Muir, Edwin. *The Present Age from 1914*. London: Cresset Press, 1939.

———. *The Structure of the Novel*. London: L. and V. Woolf, 1923.

———. *Transition. Essays on Contemporary Literature*. London: L. and V. Woolf, 1926.

Murry, J. M. *Discoveries*. London: Cape, 1930.

Myers, Walter L. *The Later Realism, a Study of Characterization in the British Novel*. Chicago: University of Chicago Press, 1927.

Nicolson, Harold. *The New Spirit in Literature*. London: British Broadcasting Corporation, 1931.

Romain, Yvonne de. "L'Évolution du roman anglais." *Revue Politique et Littéraire*, Jan. 3, 1931, pp. 13–20.

Routh, H. V. *English Literature and Ideas in the Twentieth Century*. London: Methuen, 1946.

Sackville-West, V. "The Future of the Novel." *Week-End Review*, Oct. 18, 1930, p. 535.

Schirmer, Walter F. *Der englische Roman der neuesten Zeit*. Heidelberg: C. Winter, 1923.

Scott–James, R. A. *Fifty Years of English Literature 1900–1950*. London: Longmans Green, 1951.

Simone, Irene. *Formes du roman anglais de Dickens à Joyce*. Paris: Faculté de Philosophie et Lettres, 1949.

Sitwell, Sir Osbert. "The Modern Novel: Its Cause and Cure." *Trio*, by Osbert, Edith, and Sacheverell Sitwell. London: Methuen, 1938, pp. 47–93.

Spender, Stephen. *World Within World*. New York: Harcourt, Brace, 1951.

Swinnerton, Frank. *The Georgian Scene, a Literary Panorama*. New York: Farrar and Rinehart. 1934.

Tindall, William Y. *Forces in Modern British Literature 1885–1946.* New York: Knopf, 1947.

————. "Introduction" to *The Plumed Serpent* by D. H. Lawrence. New York: Knopf, 1951, pp. v–xiv.

Van Doren, Carl, and Mark Van Doren. *American and British Literature Since 1890.* New York and London: Appleton-Century, 1939.

Vines, Sherard. *Movements in Modern English Poetry and Prose.* Tokyo: Oxford University Press, 1927.

Vowinckel, Ernst. *Der englische Roman der neuesten Zeit und Gegenwart, Stilformen und Entwicklungslinien.* Berlin: F. A. Herbig, 1926.

————. *Der englische Roman zwischen den Jahrzehnten 1927–1935.* Berlin: F. A. Herbig, 1936.

Walpole, Hugh. *Tendencies of the Modern Novel.* London: Allen and Unwin, 1934.

Ward, A. C. *Twentieth-Century Literature, 1901–1940.* London: Methuen, 1940.

Weygandt, C. *A Century of the English Novel.* New York: Century, 1925.

Wild, Friedrich. *Die englische Literatur der Gegenwart seit 1870: Drama und Roman.* Wiesbaden: Dioskurenverlag, 1928.

INDEX